Why Does My Bird Do That?

A Guide to Parrot Behavior

Why Does My Bird Do That?

A Guide to Parrot Behavior

JULIE ANN RACH

HOWELL BOOK HOUSE

Howell Book House
A Simon & Schuster Macmillan Company
1633 Broadway
New York, NY 10019-6785

Macmillan Publishing books may be purchased for business or sales promotional use.
For information please write: Special Markets Department, Macmillan Publishing USA,
1633 Broadway, New York, NY 10019-6785.

Cover Photography: Eric Ilasenko

Library of Congress Cataloging-in-Publication Data
Rach, Julie
    Why does my bird do that? / Julie Ann Rach.
        p.   cm.
    Includes bibliographical references and index.

    ISBN 0-87605-011-9

    1. Parrots—Behavior.   2. Cage birds—Behavior.   I. Title.
SF473.P3R328   1998   98-23439
636.6'8—dc21   CIP

Manufactured in the United States of America

10 9 8 7 6 5 4

DEDICATION

For my parents,
who bought me my first parakeet
and taught me to appreciate animals.

CONTENTS

The general care and first aid recommendations in this book are not intended to substitute for veterinary advice. Please consult your avian veterinarian at the first sign of illness in your pet bird.

ACKNOWLEDGMENTS

Thanks to all the bird owners who have shared their stories with me over the years. Without you, this book would not be possible.

INTRODUCTION

Parrot behavior is a subject that has fascinated researchers and frustrated bird owners for years. Researchers have long been intrigued by the natural intelligence of these clever creatures, and it's that same native intelligence and cleverness that initially charms an owner, then causes that same owner to throw up his or her hands in frustration when their birds consistently "misbehave."

Some owners have a high tolerance for parrot antics, while others do not. According to parrot behavior consultant Liz Wilson, many members of the latter group give up their parrots when the pets are about 5 years old because they just didn't realize the kinds of behaviors that normal, mature parrots are prone to.

Veterinarian Greg Harrison, coauthor of *Avian Medicine: Principles and Application,* gives us an idea of what happens to those unwanted birds: They are euthanized, sent to zoos or breeding facilities, released, abused or ignored each year because their owners cannot tolerate or change the birds' abnormal behaviors.

I can confirm that coping with an adult parrot's behaviors can try an owner's patience, sometimes severely. I've watched friends cope with bites and bruises to their fingers and their egos as their birds matured and demonstrated behavioral changes, and I learned a few things along the way about biting, screaming, sexually motivated behaviors and other potential perils of parrot ownership.

In the 10 years I've had my parrot, I've had to deal with her biting me and screaming at me out of fear, developing her confidence, improving her health and distracting her from picking her feathers, which was a long-established habit in her previous home. I also had to find ways to encourage her to eat a wider variety of healthful foods and to play with toys. At times, it would seem that we made tremendous progress, but at other times I seriously doubted I would ever make headway with all her problems.

After a few years of feeling disappointed with her progress, I realized that some of these so-called problems were far bigger issues for me than for her. I dreamed of a talking, whistling, singing, fully feathered, outwardly perfect parrot when an almost fully feathered, content bird in reasonably good health was a more realistic expectation. When I examined my own hopes, then considered the many changes that she had undergone, I readjusted my expectations and we're both much happier—I accepted her for what she was, not what I thought she should be.

Because questions concerning parrot behavior were frequently raised in many letters and phone calls I received when I was an editor at *Bird Talk* magazine, I can attest that understanding behavior is a common concern of pet bird owners. The other editors and I thought behavior was such an important topic, in fact, that we tried to include an article about behavior in each issue of the magazine, as well as providing a monthly question-and-answer column on avian behavior.

Since I've left the magazine, I've seen frequent stories in the news and documentaries on public television about research into parrot behavior, and parrot behavior conferences that bring bird owners and behavioral experts together are more popular now than they've ever been.

I hope this book will help clarify some of the mysteries of bird behavior as they relate to the kinds of birds most commonly kept as pets. To help you better understand your bird and its behavioral patterns, read on!

A Long History

Birds have been on the earth for about 140 million years. They first appeared in the late Jurassic period, and the first bird was *Archaeopteryx lithographica,* which was about the size of a crow and lived in the cycad forests.

Because bird bones are so fragile, few representatives of early birds left behind remains in the fossil record. Nevertheless, fossil remains have been found that indicate that birds were on the scene during the Eocene epoch, which occurred about 55 million years ago.

The earliest fossil parrot may be *Archaeopsittacus verreauxi* from the lower Miocene period of about 30 million years ago. It was described from a bone found in France. Some experts believe that this particular specimen is not a parrot, however, and that the first fossil parrot was *Conuropsis fratercula,* fossils of which were found in Nebraska. *Conuropsis fratercula* lived about 20 million years ago. Representatives of the *Pionus* and *Aratinga* genera were in existence less than one million years ago.

Now that we have established the beginnings of parrots, let's look back at the beginnings of the association between people and parrots. The ancient Egyptians are credited as being the first people to keep birds, particularly pigeons. Queen Hatsheput (1504 to 1482 B.C.) is said to be the first monarch to create a royal zoo, which included exotic birds. The ancient Persians also knew about talking birds as early as the fifth century B.C., when a court physician and naturalist wrote about talking birds that were described to him by Indian merchants.

From Egypt, bird keeping spread to Greece and Rome. Alexander the Great receives credit from some historians with discovering the Alexandrine parakeet,

Keeping canaries became popular among wealthy Europeans during the Renaissance. (PHOTO BY ERIC ILASENKO)

and the Greeks are credited with popularizing parrot keeping outside of the birds' native lands of Africa and Asia.

Well-to-do Romans built extensive garden aviaries, and they also employed mockingbirds in the entryways of their homes as feathered doorbells that would announce visitors. The Romans are also thought to be the first bird dealers, bringing different types of birds to Great Britain and the European continent.

Until the Renaissance, bird keeping was considered a hobby that only the wealthy could pursue. After canaries were introduced to Europe by Portuguese sailors, bird keeping began to flourish, although it was still confined largely to upper-class fanciers. Spanish monks began to propagate canaries for the royal families of Europe and other wealthy bird fanciers. The monks tried to keep tight control over their birds, only allowing the males to be exported, but somehow female canaries made it to other parts of Europe. By the 1600s, the Dutch were producing show canaries. Some of these birds were exported to Britain, and bird keeping began to be more accessible to the masses.

At about the same time, in the British penal colony of Australia, a forger named Thomas Watling first described the budgerigar's ability to mimic human speech. This bird was able to greet Watling's employer by saying "How do you do, Dr. White?"

Bird keeping as we know it today can trace its beginnings to Victorian Great Britain, when bird sellers in the British Isles would offer goldfinches and larks to ship captains en route to the West Indies. These common European birds would then be traded in the islands for species found commonly there.

In the United States, bird keeping began to boom after World War II. The budgie rose to its position as most popular pet bird in the 1950s, and the bird care industry began to grow steadily and significantly in the 1980s.

What began as a few companies packaging bird seed and selling cages soon grew to a multifaceted industry that provides a variety of foods, cages, treats, toys, grooming utensils, talking tapes and compact discs, books and videotapes on bird care, veterinary specialization and behavioral counseling for both pets and owners.

A Wild Harvest

At the start, parrot keeping depended heavily upon trapping parrots in the wild to turn them into pets. Until the late 1970s, this procedure was accepted as the normal way of procuring a bird. At this point in time, some forward-thinking parrot keepers began to set up pairs of commonly imported species to produce parrots specifically for the pet trade.

By the 1980s, some species, such as sun and jenday conures, were bred with regularity in captivity. These domestically bred birds had all the exotic appeal of their wild-caught cousins without some of the common behavior problems, such as fear biting, screaming or hiding in the corner of the cage. The pet-owning public began to respond to these domestically bred birds, and breeders turned their attention to other species. Wild-caught parrots still dominated the market, however.

When parrots were caught in the wild and imported into the United States and Europe in great numbers, nets, snares and other methods were used to trap the birds, which were usually enticed to the capture site with a lure bird that had been tied or glued to the spot by the trappers. In some cases, nesting trees were cut down and parent birds killed while trappers robbed the nest of chicks. Birds were taken from the jungle to holding stations, from which they were exported.

Along the way, these captured birds were fed whatever food happened to be available with little concern shown for proper parrot nutrition. The food that the birds received in captivity may or may not have been what they were used to in the jungle, and some of the birds died from the different diet or from the stress of being captured.

If birds were injured in the capture process, little to no veterinary care was available to them. Many died from their injuries, while others were crippled for life. Once in the country of export, birds were held at import stations to ensure that they did not carry any communicable diseases, such as Newcastle disease, and then they were distributed to pet stores.

The birds that survived all this were stressed, to say the least. As wild animals snatched from the jungle, they hadn't the foggiest notion of how to be pets or what humans expected of them. Humans had, after all, taken them from their familiar surroundings and hurt many of them along the way—why should these intelligent, sensitive creatures want to associate with the humans who would buy them as pets?

As a result, these wild-caught birds often made less-than-desirable pets. They screamed, they bit, they pulled their feathers or they cowered in the corners of their cages. My own parrot did all these things when I first adopted her, and it took six years of constant care on my part and the efforts of several avian veterinarians and behaviorists to restore her health and to curtail her feather-picking and biting habits.

Early taming procedures for wild-caught birds were fairly brutal. Trainers often encouraged owners to break their birds' spirits by handling the birds with heavy gloves, throwing the birds on the ground, striking the birds' cages or even worse, striking the birds themselves. Not surprisingly, many of these untamed birds became even more impossible to handle. Some particularly incorrigible specimens were labeled broncos, with the implication that they, like the wild horses they were named for, would never be tamed.

Some breeders took these unhandleable birds and set them up in breeding programs, where some of the birds proved to be suitable parents. Breeders pulled some of the chicks and hand-raised them to improve the chicks' pet qualities, and, in time, domestic-bred birds largely replaced wild-caught birds in the pet market.

A Better Option

In the early 1990s, the importation of parrots was outlawed in the United States, so domestic-bred birds were the primary option available to most people seeking a parrot, although some wild-caught adults were still offered for sale by owners who were unable to turn these birds into the loving pets they desired. Because the domestic-bred birds bonded with humans almost from the instant they hatched, they made much better pets than their wild-caught counterparts. And because breeders wanted to ensure their livelihood for the future, the domestic-bred birds were healthier than their wild-caught brethren, too, which also helped make them more suitable pets.

Domestic-bred birds still needed behavior modification from time to time, but fortunately, kinder, gentler methods of reprimanding birds that occasionally got out of hand were now touted by parrot behavior consultants. These included "time-outs" similar to those given to unruly children, stern tones of voice or praising good behavior instead of punishing misbehavior. Owners now took the time to see things from the birds' point of view, which helped them better understand some behaviors that had been considered problems (by people), but were perfectly normal for the birds.

In *The Pet Bird Handbook,* Patricia Sutherland writes that: "Understanding basic bird behavior is one of the best ways to develop 'bird sense'—a special brand of the more common 'common sense.' Knowing what makes our feathered friends tick is essential to taming and proper handling." It also makes the relationship you develop with your pet more enjoyable for both of you.

chapter 1

FLOCK BEHAVIOR IN THE WILD AND HOW IT APPLIES IN THE HOME

To understand parrot behavior in the home, one must first start in the jungle. Parrots can be found in the wild on the continents of North America, South America, Australia, Africa and Asia, and on some islands in the Caribbean and the South Pacific.

Most of the species are confined to relatively small areas of the world. Brazil, for example, is home to 70 parrot species, while Australia is home to another 52. Colombia and Venezuela are home to 49 and 48 species, respectively, and New Guinea is home to an additional 46 species.

Parrot lovers who want to witness behaviors in a natural setting can visit the Tambopata Research Center in southeastern Peru. The center, which has been in operation since 1990, is located near Manu National Park, where Charles Munn of the Wildlife Conservation Society has been studying the habits of wild macaws, particularly as they apply to a clay lick in the park.

Visitors to Tambopata can see macaws at the clay lick, as well as macaws and other parrots in the jungle surrounding the center. Some of these birds are macaws that the research center staff hand-fed, then released back to the wild. These birds are still tame enough to willingly approach staff members and visitors.

In addition to providing an eco-tourism opportunity for bird lovers, the research center is devoted to improving the reproductive rates of macaws in the area. It has done this by providing additional artificial nesting sites and by studying growth rates and other predictors of survival in chicks. Staff members have also removed some chicks from the nests, hand-fed them and returned them to the wild as noted earlier. They hope someday to be able to apply the lessons learned about parrot reproduction to other parrot species in the area.

If you don't want to travel to Peru and you live in a temperate climate, you may be able to see feral parrots in your area. Los Angeles area bird-watchers may have the chance to observe psittacine behavior in the wilds of canyons, parks and residential streets because feral flocks of conures (cherry heads, mitreds and nandays are the most frequently seen species), Amazons and other psittacine species have been reported in the area.

Bird lovers from the Pacific Palisades to Pasadena have been delighted by the antics of these feral birds, which regularly perform gymnastic routines on power lines or raid nut trees. The birds stay in an area for a few days, then move over a few city blocks to start the routine over again.

Another flock of conures has been reported on Telegraph Hill in San Francisco, and flocks of feral parrots may exist in the San Diego area of southern California, Texas, Florida and other temperate climate zones. Feral flocks of Quaker parrots have been reported in less-temperate climates, such as Seattle and the New England region.

How these parrots got loose is anyone's guess—some attribute the birds to a pet store fire, while others say that a smuggler who was about to be captured freed his supply of birds. Still others with a more realistic attitude attribute their presence to a great many lost (or intentionally freed) pets who were lucky enough to escape predators and band together.

Wherever they live in the world, parrots are naturally social creatures and live together in flocks ranging from a few individuals to several hundred birds. Lowland tropical rain forest is the most typical habitat for parrots, but they can also be found in semiarid climates, mountain areas or savannahs. Some species are even seen in parks and other urban environments in South America and Australia.

Certain species are found in specialized wild habitats, such as Australia's ground parrot that is found in a very restricted mountain heath area in southern Australia. Others, such as Arizona's thickbilled parrots, glossy cockatoos or Tucuman Amazons, seem to live in habitats that contain a particular foodstuff that the parrots enjoy.

Some species adapt in different ways to different environments. For example, budgerigars that live in central Australia have adapted to the harshness of the environment by reproducing at young ages and having many chicks in the hope that some will survive the rigors of life in this part of the country. Budgies that live on the coast and in the central southern areas, where the climate is less extreme, do not demonstrate this ability to breed early and often.

In the wild, another Australian species, the cockatiel, is active during the early morning and the late afternoon. These are the times when the birds usually head toward a water source to drink, being sure to land, drink and leave quickly, rather than become a meal for a passing bird of prey. They spend a good bit of their days on the ground, searching for food, but they are likely to spend midday blending into their surroundings by sitting lengthwise along tree branches, usually dead limbs that are free of foliage.

Most parrots eat seeds and different types of fruits that they find in the treetops or on the ground. Many medium- and large-sized parrot species use one foot (usually the left) to pick up and hold food while they are eating.

To open a seed, a bird uses its tongue to steady the seed against the underside of its upper beak (a parrot's upper beak has ridges in it that help hold food steady) and peels away the seed husk with its sharp lower beak.

Some parrots, such as lories and lorikeets, are specialized feeders. These brush-tongued parrots live strictly in trees, where they feed on nectar, pollen and soft fruits.

Some species actually change their diets significantly in the wild when the opportunity is right. For example, the kea parrot of New Zealand changed its diet from fruits and seeds to lamb after settlers in the area began raising sheep. The importance of lamb in the kea's diet has been overemphasized by some, so much so that a bounty was paid on keas in the past. According to Joseph Forshaw's *Parrots of the World,* these large, stocky parrots only feed on sheep trapped in snow, sick or injured animals or animals the birds perceive as dead. Keas are now under limited protection of the New Zealand government.

A Daily Routine

In the wild, the flocks greet the dawn by vocalizing. They do this to alert members of the flock that they will be moving soon, and they also let other flocks in the area know where they are. After the flock is awake, they move from their roosting trees to find food.

Bird language in the wild includes calls to signal the flock that food has been found, calls that indicate a mate has been won, calls that indicate danger is near, calls that bring the flock together at the end of a day, songs to establish territories and to attract mates and chattering that some researchers believe resembles human conversation.

The birds forage and eat throughout the day, alerting other members of the flock to their location and to potential dangers through a series of calls and other vocalizations.

When they aren't foraging or eating, parrots in the wild spend a good part of their day playing. Young birds learn about their environment through play, and older birds use the opportunity to play to exercise and to reaffirm their position in the flock.

As the day ends, the birds call to each other to gather flock members together, and the flock goes back to roost, starting the cycle again in the morning.

Parrots become sexually mature at around 2 years of age for smaller species and at around 3 years of age for larger species. For humans, differentiating between the sexes is often difficult because males and females frequently look the same. An exception to this rule is the eclectus, in which males are green and females are purple and red. The extreme difference in the coloring of the sexes, which is called sexual dimorphism, led early scientists to believe that they had actually discovered two different species of parrots!

Most psittacine species are monogamous, and many mate for long periods, perhaps for life. Pairs demonstrate pair-bonding behavior, such as mutual preening or sitting very close to one another, throughout the year. Experts believe that a strong pair bond helps parent birds be more successful at laying fertile eggs and raising chicks.

A variety of conditions, including rainfall, an increase in the food supply and gradually longer days, stimulate parrots to breed in their natural environments. In breeding facilities and pet homes, owners will notice that their birds begin to go into breeding mode in the late winter, spring or summer. Few parrots are year-round breeders.

In the wild, parrots nest in tree cavities, termite mounds, niches carved in faces of sandstone cliffs and other natural crevices. Few parrots excavate a nest from scratch, according to parrot expert Joseph Forshaw, but they will enlarge or expand an existing nest site that has been abandoned by other species of birds.

Parrot chicks are altricial when they hatch, meaning that they are blind, featherless and helpless. However, by the time they are about 3 weeks old, like these cockatiel chicks, their eyes have opened and they have started to develop feathers. (PHOTO BY GARY A. GALLERSTEIN, DVM)

The nests are predominantly enclosed and parrot eggs are most typically white. They can, therefore, easily be seen by a parent bird in the darkness of the nesting chamber. Clutch size ranges from two to five eggs for larger species, and it can be as large as eight for smaller species. Eggs are laid on an approximately every-other-day schedule. The incubation period ranges from 14 to more than 30 days.

Newly hatched young are altricial. This means they are blind, naked and completely dependent upon their parents. A chick's eyes open about two weeks after hatching, and chicks stay in the nest for three weeks to three months, with smaller species leaving the nest sooner than their larger cousins.

As a rule, parrots do not build what we think of as nests. An exception to this rule is the Quaker, or monk, parrot, which can build quite elaborate nests out of sticks.

From the Treetop to the Cagetop

What does all this mean to a parrot owner? Whether they are in the jungle or in your living room, parrots demonstrate some similar behaviors. They eat and play, they call to mates and other flock members and they vocalize at sunrise and sunset. These are all normal behaviors that are unlikely to be modified significantly, although you can usually work with your parrot to modulate its noise level.

Parrots, whether in the wild or in your home, communicate by whistling and vocalizing. Often, vocalizing crosses the line into screaming or loudly speaking the phrases you have so lovingly taught your bird, if you are fortunate enough to have a talking parrot. While these sounds may be music to your ears, your neighbors (especially if you're in an apartment or condominium) may not find your pet's antics so charming.

If noise is a concern, do not select a cockatoo or a macaw for your pet because these two species are among the noisiest of parrots. Cockatoos often greet the dawn by screaming, and some feel compelled to acknowledge sunset in the same way. Certain species, such as Moluccans, may hoot and stamp their feet as part of their natural display. Macaws' screams are higher pitched than cockatoos, which may make them even more grating on your ears or those of your neighbors.

Cockatoos in general like to be the life of the party and the center of their owners' universe. They are emotionally needy birds that require a great deal of time and attention from their owners. If they do not receive it, cockatoos can become destructive feather pickers—some even turn to self-mutilation.

For those considering a medium-sized parrot, keep in mind that Amazons, although lively clowns, can whistle and scream frequently throughout the day. The good news is that their noise level should not bother neighbors. How you

If your bird spends time on the floor in your home, you must be careful that you don't step on it or that it doesn't injure itself by chewing something that it shouldn't. (PHOTO BY JULIE RACH)

feel about sharing space with a noisy green parrot is another matter. For close quarters where noise may be a factor, choose a smaller bird, such as a parakeet, lory or African grey.

For those of you concerned about chewing, realize that all parrots chew to some extent. However, some species, such as conures, are more voracious than others. By providing your parrot with access to appropriate chewables, such as food, nuts or toys, you fulfill its need to chew while reducing the possibility of your bird chewing on some of your possessions.

Another behavior that concerns new parrot owners is biting. If you start with a young bird and handle it properly, you should not be bitten too often, but you must realize that being bitten is part of parrot ownership and, as a longtime bird-owning friend of mine once put it, "Nobody ever died from a bird bite."

Some parrots are more prone to biting during certain times of the year, such as breeding season, or they are incited to bite by their owners roughhousing with them. By being careful in the way you handle your bird, you will significantly reduce your chances of being bitten.

If space is a concern, I would recommend eliminating the large parrots, such as macaws and cockatoos, from consideration. These birds, kept in

Parrots, such as this bare-eyed cockatoo, will sometimes eliminate in their food or water dishes. Be careful when placing bowls in your bird's cage or when placing your bird on a T-stand. (PHOTO BY GARY A. GALLERSTEIN, DVM)

appropriate-sized cages, can occupy as much space as a full-size refrigerator! If these large parrots are not allowed the opportunity to exercise outside their cages, they may develop some behavior problems, such as screaming or biting.

Remember that your bird needs the largest cage you can afford in order to benefit from daily exercise. The cage you select should be large enough so your bird can fully extend its wings without having the wings touch the sides of the cage. The bird should also have ample clearance for its head from the cage ceiling and its tail from the cage floor when sitting on its perch. In addition to your bird, the cage must hold a few perches, some toys, a food bowl, a water bowl and possibly a bathtub.

When choosing your bird's cage, keep in mind that pet birds are like little airplanes, flying an area, rather than little helicopters that hover up and down. For this reason, long rectangular cages that offer horizontal space for short flights are preferred to tall cages that don't provide much flying room. All cage birds—finches, canaries, softbills and parrots—have the need to fly across their cages, so make a long rectangular cage a priority regardless of the species you keep.

When setting up a cage for a young parrot, you may want to keep the perches fairly low. Some young birds, particularly African greys, are notoriously clumsy when they're first getting the hang of perching and climbing. Once you see that your bird is navigating around the cage with ease, you can raise the perch heights.

When placing perches in your bird's cage, try to vary the heights slightly so your bird has different "levels" in its cage. Vary the diameters slightly, too, so your bird can exercise its feet by sitting on a perch of recommended size part of the time and on one that's slightly larger than the recommended diameter the rest of the time.

Recommended perch diameters are as follows: $3/8$ inch for finches and canaries, $1/2$ inch for budgies, $5/8$ inch for cockatiels, $3/4$ inch for conures, 1 inch for Amazons and other medium-sized parrots and 2 inches for cockatoos and macaws.

Don't place any perches over food or water dishes because birds can and will contaminate food or water by eliminating in it. Finally, place one perch higher than the rest for a nighttime sleeping roost. Parrots like to sleep on the highest point they can find to perch, so please provide this security to your pet.

Domed or round cages may cause some birds to develop behavioral problems, such as screaming, feather chewing or self-mutilation because they feel uneasy without a corner to settle into. This information helped me to better understand my parrot's situation in her previous home. She had lived in a large, round, domed cage, and she chewed her feathers. She now lives in a smaller, rectangular cage and doesn't pick her feathers. I believe she didn't feel completely comfortable in her old cage because it was difficult for her to get around in, given her crippled legs and reduced mobility. In her present cage, she can maneuver quite well and, I would surmise, feels more at ease.

As you select a cage, you'll need to keep in mind one other dimension: bar spacing. This is the distance between the cage bars, and it's important because birds can get themselves stuck between the bars or even escape from a cage if the bar spacing isn't right for them.

Here are the recommended bar spacing for commonly kept pet birds: budgies/parakeets, canaries, finches and lovebirds, $3/8$ inch; cockatiels and small conures, $1/2$ to $3/4$ inch; Amazons, African greys and other medium-sized parrots, $3/4$ to 1 inch; macaws and cockatoos, $3/4$ to $1^1/2$ inches.

Reject any cages that have sharp interior wires that could poke your bird. Also be aware that birds may injure themselves on ornate scrollwork that decorates some cages.

If you are choosing a cage for a parrot, make sure the cage you choose has some horizontal bars in it so your bird will be able to climb the cage walls if it wants to exercise. Climbing is good exercise that helps a parrot burn off energy it might otherwise use to scream or bite or pull its feathers, so be sure to encourage your pet to exercise inside its cage and out of it. Finches, canaries and softbills are

Parrots like to climb. Be sure to provide your pet with climbing opportunities in your home. (PHOTO BY JULIE RACH)

more apt to hop and flit across the cage than they are to climb the cage walls, so horizontal bars are not as great a requirement for them as they are for hookbilled birds.

If you find wooden or bamboo cages in your shopping excursions for a parrot cage, reject them immediately unless the wood is lined with wire or wire mesh. Although they may be suitable for finches and songbirds, a busy hookbill beak will soon make short work of a wooden or bamboo cage, and you'll be left with the problem of finding a new home for your pet!

Some birds have special caging requirements. My parrot, for example, lives in a rectangular rabbit cage because it has smaller mesh that she can hook her beak into easily. This helps her, with her physical limitations, get around more quickly.

A budgie I know named Calvin was handicapped as a chick. (I think his mother sat on him too tightly in the nest and squashed his developing skeleton a bit.) As a result of injuries he suffered early in life, Calvin didn't perch too well and had trouble getting around in and living in a conventional wire bird cage. His owner searched through pet stores to find the best cage for her physically challenged pet, and her solution was a wire hamster cage with climbing ramps and resting platforms, rather than traditional perches. Because the platforms and ramps were wide and had both horizontal and vertical bars on them, Calvin could maneuver around his cage pretty well.

You'll probably notice that your bird spends a lot of time moving around its cage. This mimics the movements of flocks in the wild. During these movements, it often uses its beak as much as its feet. Parrots are very good at using their beaks to climb, reach, hold, bite, hang, eat, preen or play, depending on what their current activities call for.

In your home, your parrot probably won't spend much time foraging for its food. To provide an outlet for those foraging tendencies, consider offering food in different forms from time to time. Offer whole green beans or peas in the pod to encourage your bird to work for its food a little bit. You can also give your bird nuts in the shell to challenge its mind as well as nourish its body.

To further help your bird expend the energy it would use to forage and feed in the wild, give it ample opportunities to play. Busy, occupied birds are less likely to misbehave, and they become well-adjusted, content companions. Birds that might otherwise scream, pull their feathers or become aggressive can channel their energies into play if provided with the chance.

Parrots need suitable toys to play with. If you try one type of toy—for example, a chain with a bell on it—and your bird doesn't like it, don't give up! You may have to try several different types of toys before you find one that your bird likes.

In her previous home, my bird had toys with bells on them and lava rocks hung on chains. While some parrots might find them suitable, she did not, and she did not play much. I had to try a variety of toys—some colorful wooden ones, some rope toys, some with intricate networks of leather thongs—in order to find some that she liked. Her favorite type of toy is one that she can chew on and

Toys can be colorful or plain, complicated or simple. You will have to determine which type is right for your bird. (Photo by Julie Rach)

You can encourage your bird to play by challenging it to a game of tug-of-war. (Photo by Julie Rach)

destroy, but the chewable items can be parrot cookies, soft wood or leather thongs. Her tastes and interests change, so I have to rotate the toys in her cage regularly to keep her interested in them.

Some birds do not react well to brightly colored toys, while others love them. A friend who has a flock of three birds reports that her pets seem to favor toys that have colors similar to those of the birds' plumage. Perhaps these birds perceive items of a similar color as less threatening than those that are brightly colored and foreign to them.

In addition to playing with toys, your parrot needs a chance to flap its wings, climb, hang off of a perch or play gym or chase a ball. All these activities will help your pet burn off energy. Again, each parrot will have activities that it prefers, so you will have to see which type of exercise appeals to your parrot.

Remember to take time to play with your bird, too. Parrots are flock animals, so your bird would naturally expect to have some company while it's playing. You can roll your bird over and pet its "tickle spots," you can play tug-of-war with it, you can introduce it to a new toy or you can hold it on your hand or arm while it flaps.

chapter 2

PARROT BEHAVIOR EXAMINED

Parrot behavior has been studied in a laboratory setting for almost 50 years. Today, however, it's difficult to discuss parrot behavior without mentioning an amazing African grey parrot who's been the subject of study by an evolutionary biologist for more than 20 years.

Alex the Grey

In 1977, Irene Pepperberg, PhD, purchased an African grey parrot selected at random from the birds at a Chicago pet store as part of a research project to examine animal intelligence and communication skills.

That bird is Alex, and he has proved to be an exceptional research subject in the ensuing years. Dr. Pepperberg has learned that Alex not only uses human language to communicate, but he uses language appropriately. Alex is able to note differences and similarities in objects that are shown to him and to tell researchers the colors of the objects and the materials from which they are made.

In addition, Alex asks for toys or treats in the course of his day at the lab or to be carried from one part of the lab to another, and he tells researchers "No!" forcefully if they bring him the wrong treat or toy or if they try to set him down in a part of the lab he didn't ask to visit.

Alex also apologizes to people in the laboratory if he bites them (although he is likely to bite them again). When Dr. Pepperberg left Alex at a veterinary hospital for surgery, he said to her, "Come here. I love you. I'm sorry. I want to go back." Apparently, Alex thought he was being punished by being left at the hospital.

Alex spends about eight hours a day in a lab room with researchers and is confined to a roomy cage when he is alone. His diet consists of water and a standard parrot seed mix, supplemented with fresh vegetables, fruits and treats such as cashews, almonds, pecans and walnuts.

When he responds to a question about an object correctly, Alex often receives the object to play with as a reward for giving the right answer. If he does not answer correctly, he is told to try again or to give a better response. If he asks for a treat by name, he is given that treat immediately after he answers the trainer's question correctly.

In 1992, two African grey chicks joined Alex in the laboratory. These birds began by identifying objects, such as paper or cork. Then they learned to distinguish items, including the number of a particular item, its relative size, the material it is made from and its color. Finally, the birds learn phonemes (distinctive sounds) and how to combine them.

Alex and the other birds in Dr. Pepperberg's lab are not the first African greys studied in this manner. Researchers in Europe developed a method of communicating with African greys in the 1940s and 1950s, and a German researcher popularized the use of the model/rival technique to teach and study African grey parrots.

In the model/rival method, the teacher shows one of two students (either avian or human) an object and asks what it is. If the student identifies it correctly, the teacher gives the object to the student to examine and play with. If the student gives an incorrect answer, the teacher and the other student "model" the correct response, then the teacher asks the first student the question again. Tests conducted on Alex indicate that he can answer 80 percent of the questions asked him correctly.

Dr. Pepperberg became interested in studying animal intelligence in 1973 while completing her doctorate in chemical physics at Harvard. After seeing the success others had in teaching chimps to use sign language, she began studying animal intelligence with a special emphasis on vocal communication. She spent about 40 hours each week researching animal intelligence while devoting another 40 hours a week to completing her doctorate.

In the course of her research, Dr. Pepperberg read reports in which psychologists had studied parrots' abilities to solve problems and to communicate. She believed that earlier investigations had failed to achieve meaningful communication with their study subjects because of inappropriate training practices and set out to test her theory with Alex, a borrowed laboratory, some volunteer assistants and some used equipment.

Within two years of beginning her study, Dr. Pepperberg could show that Alex used language with meaning to identify objects. He could identify more than 30 items by name, shape and color and had averaged 80 percent accuracy on tests administered to chart his progress.

Alex now knows the names of almost 100 items, he can count to six, he can name about seven colors and about seven different types of materials. He has also made up his own names for some items, such as "banana cracker" to describe a banana chip, "cork nut" to ask for an almond in its shell and "rock corn" to distinguish dried corn from fresh. Depending on his level of interest on a given day, Alex's attention span ranges from a few minutes to more than two hours.

From the beginning of the study, Alex has been allowed regular interaction and cuddling with Dr. Pepperberg and her student assistants. They believe this interaction mimics the attention Alex would receive from his flockmates. They also think this attention is vital to Alex's success and to getting him to cooperate in the research project. Alex has a method of testing new students in the program: He rattles off a list of items that he desires, sending the student scrambling to fetch what may end up being dozens of foods and toys. To some, it seems as though Alex wants to know if the new person speaks the same language as he does.

At the beginning of the study, Alex was approximately 1 year old and had received no prior speech instruction. He was domestically bred, but he was not a hand-raised parrot. The chicks that joined the study in 1992 were domestically bred and hand-raised.

In 1997, research involving Alex was discussed at the annual American Veterinary Medical Association meeting. After administering intelligence tests used on dolphins and chimps, Dr. Pepperberg announced that Alex scored as well as they did on many of them, and better than some. This means that Alex is capable of mastering complex intellectual concepts that humans cannot achieve until they are 5 years of age.

The Parrot's Brain

Although the term "birdbrain" is not usually a compliment, Alex has demonstrated that a bird's brain is really capable of quite amazing feats. Parrots have one of the largest brains in the class *Aves*. They are thought to have large brains because they need to forage for food in the wild. Their large brains also help them function in flock situations, allowing them to learn from other parrots, which helps them have a better chance of survival.

Parrot brains differ from mammal brains in several ways, according to Bonnie Munro Doane. The major differences are found in the sizes of the cerebral cortex and the striatum. In mammals, the cortex is large and the striatum is small. In parrots, the reverse is true. The striatum is the center of birds' intelligence. Although parrots use a different part of their brains than we do to think, it is apparent that they, indeed, have the capability to process information and use it intelligently.

Researcher Theodore X. Barber, PhD, came to the following conclusions regarding birds, which he shared in *The Human Nature of Birds,* after analyzing data on bird migration, avian learning abilities and avian behavior:

One researcher has discovered that playing joyfully is a behavior that birds and people have in common.
(PHOTO BY JULIE RACH)

1. Birds have many abilities that humans assume are unique to humans, such as musical ability, the ability to form abstract concepts, the ability to use intelligence to cope with changing life demands and the ability to play with joy and mate erotically.

2. While humans are superior to birds in some kinds of intelligence (i.e., symbolic-linguistic intelligence), birds are superior to humans in other types of intelligence (i.e., navigational intelligence).

3. Birds are not only intelligent, aware and willful; they can also communicate meaningfully with humans and relate to them as close, caring friends.

Parrot owners can certainly agree with Barber's first conclusion. Some parrots are composers of music, whether it be songs or whistles. Parrots demonstrate the ability to use their intelligence to meet the demands of living, and they certainly know how to play with joy. Just watch a cockatoo taking apart a complicated toy or see a budgie chattering happily to its reflection in a mirror—those are both joyful experiences for bird and owner.

If parrots can play joyfully, can they also express other emotions? I believe that they can. My parrot shows different emotions, and I can tell when she is happy or when she's angry with me. I can also sense when she's bored or when something frightens her. She reacts to my emotions, getting quiet and cuddly when I am sad or loud and boisterous when I am enjoying a television program or chatting with good friends on the phone.

Researchers in the wild have seen examples of what could be described as birds mourning when their mates are taken by birds of prey or struck by cars. These birds have been seen huddling close to their dead mates, and some attempt to lift the dead birds' bodies with their own wings as if encouraging the lost mate to fly away with them.

Some parrots that have lost their longtime owners seem to become depressed after their owners' deaths. They stop eating for awhile, lose interest in their surroundings and neglect their grooming habits, such as feather preening. If you acquire a parrot that has recently lost its owner, give the bird time and space to grieve. Understand that not only has it lost a very good friend, its whole world and routine have been turned upside down, and the new situation with you will take some adjustment.

Try to encourage a grieving parrot to eat and make it feel as if it is part of your family, but don't expect it to get over the loss quickly. In time, the bird should be able to form a bond with you or with someone in your family, but it has to mourn first. While the bird is mourning, make sure it does not spend excessive amounts of time in its cage. Too much in-cage time can cause a bird to develop problems relating to territory and space.

Barber's third conclusion is indisputable to parrot owners. We know that our birds can communicate with us, whether they choose to use our language or opt to teach us theirs. Our parrots certainly can read our moods as well as some of our friends do, and they are always there for us, sometimes when no one else can be—at the end of a long, difficult day, in the middle of the night when we've had a bad dream or on New Year's Eve when all our human friends are out on the town.

Barber points out that birds communicate non-verbally with each other using mouth motions, feather raising, neck stretching, crouching, leaping and fluttering. Pet birds may use some of these communications skills with the human members of their flock. See how many of these behaviors your bird demonstrates in the course of a day—you may be surprised!

For even more fun, try answering your bird in its language and see what response you get. I play along with my bird and mimic the clicks, whistles and whirrs she makes, which seems to please her greatly. She pins her eyes and fluffs her feathers and makes more noises, which I try to answer.

Pet Bird Behavior Compared

Certain personality characteristics are shared by particular species of commonly kept cage birds. The following chart can be used to determine the characteristics that are important to you, which may in turn help you to select a pet bird that you will enjoy.

Know from the start that all parrots will occasionally scream, bite, chew or otherwise misbehave from a human point of view. The goal of a good parrot-owner relationship is to minimize the number of episodes of misbehavior that a bird is involved in each day.

More information about the different types of pet birds is available in Appendix A, "Pet Bird Personalities."

Pet Bird Behavior

Species	Activity level	Noise level	Playfulness	Destructiveness
African Greys	Moderate	Moderate	Moderate	Moderate
Amazons	High	Moderate to high	High	Moderate to high
Brotogeris	Moderate	Moderate to high	Moderate to high	Low
Budgerigars	High	Low	High	Low
Caiques	High	Low to moderate	High	Low to moderate
Canaries	Low to moderate	Low	Low	Low
Cockatiels	Moderate to high	Low to moderate	Moderate	Low
Cockatoos	High	High to extremely high	High	Moderate to high
Conures	High	Moderate to high	Moderate to high	Moderate to high
Diamond Doves	Low	Low	Low	Low
Eclectus	Low to moderate	Moderate	Low	Moderate
Finches	High	Low	Low	Low
Grass Parakeets	High	Low	Low	Low
Hawkheaded Parrots	Moderate	Moderate to high	High	Moderate
Kakarikis	High	Moderate	High	Moderate

Cuddly?	Require regular interaction with owners?	Shoulder bird?	Talking potential	Biting potential
Possibly	Yes	Possibly	High	Moderate
Low to moderate	Yes	Possibly	Moderate to high	High to extremely high
Moderate to high	Yes	Possibly	Moderate	Moderate
Moderate	If kept as single pet, yes.	Yes	High	Low
Possibly	Yes	Yes	Low	Low
No	No	Possibly	Low	Low
Possibly	If kept as single pet, yes.	Yes	Low	Moderate
Yes	Yes	No	Low	High
Possibly	Yes	Possibly	Low	Moderate
No	No	No	Low	Low
No	Yes	No	Low to moderate	Moderate
No	No	No	Low	Low
No	No	No	Low	Low
Possibly	Yes	Possibly	Low to moderate	Moderate
No	No	No	Low	Low to moderate

continues

Pet Bird Behavior *continued*

Species	Activity level	Noise level	Playfulness	Destructiveness
Lories	Moderate to high	Moderate	High	Low to moderate
Lovebirds	High	Low	Moderate to high	Low
Macaws	Moderate to high	High	High	High
Mynahs	Moderate	High	Moderate	Low
Parrotlets	High	Moderate	Moderate	Low to moderate
Pekin Robins	High	Low	Low	Low
Pionus	Low	Moderate	Moderate	Low to moderate
Quaker Parrots	Moderate to high	Moderate to high	Moderate to high	Moderate
Ringnecks	Moderate to high	Moderate to high	Moderate	Moderate
Rosellas	Moderate	Low	Moderate	Low
Senegals	High	Moderate	Moderate to high	Low to moderate
Tanygnathus	Low	Moderate	Low	Moderate to high
Toucans	High	Moderate to high	Low	Low
Touracos	Moderate	High	Low	Low

Cuddly?	Require regular interaction with owners?	Shoulder bird?	Talking potential	Biting potential
No	Yes	Possibly	Moderate	Moderate
No	If kept as single pet, yes.	Possibly	Low	Moderate
Possibly	Yes	No	Low to moderate	High
No	Yes	Yes	High	Low
Possibly	If kept as single pet, yes.	Yes	Low	Moderate
No	No	No	Low	Low
Possibly	Yes	Yes	Low	Low
Possibly	Yes	Yes	Moderate to high	Low to moderate
Possibly	Yes	Possibly	Moderate to high	Moderate
No	Yes	No	Moderate	Low
Possibly	Yes	Possibly	Low	Low
Possibly	No	No	Low	Low
No	No	No	Low	Low
No	No	No	Low	Low

How to Select a Parrot

Parrots can be purchased through several sources, including classified newspaper advertisements, bird shows and marts and pet stores. Each source provides advantages and disadvantages.

Classified Advertisements

Classified advertisements are usually placed by private parties who want to place pets in new homes. If the advertiser offers young birds, you've undoubtedly found a private breeder who wants to place a few birds in good homes. Some breeders may also offer older birds for sale. These are most likely breeder birds that are too old to produce chicks but that are still good candidates for pet situations.

If you buy your bird from a private breeder, you will probably be shown only the birds that the breeder has for sale. Do not be offended or upset if you cannot see all the birds that the breeder keeps; some birds are sensitive about the presence of strangers during breeding season, and sensitive birds may destroy eggs or kill chicks when they're upset. If, however, a breeder is willing to show you around his or her facility, consider it a special treat and an honor that few people have bestowed on them.

Bird Shows and Bird Marts

Bird shows and marts offer bird breeders and bird buyers an opportunity to get together to share a love for birds. Bird shows can provide prospective bird owners with the chance to see many different types of birds in one place (usually far more than many pet shops would keep at a time), which can help you narrow your choices if you're undecided about which species to keep.

A bird mart is a little different from a bird show. At a bird mart, various species of birds and a wide variety of bird keeping supplies are offered for sale, so you can go and shop to your heart's content.

Pet Stores

Pet stores may or may not be the ideal place to purchase a parrot. You'll have to check with stores in your area to determine if they even sell pets because many stores discontinued selling livestock in the early 1990s. These stores will be listed as "pet supply stores" in your phone book and may be the places you'll want to go to get the cage, food, dishes, perches, toys and other accessories you'll need before your bird comes home.

If a store in your area sells live pets, you'll need to visit the store and make sure it's clean and well kept. Walk around the store a bit. Are the floors clean? Do the cages look and smell as though they're cleaned regularly? Do the animals in the cages appear alert, well fed and healthy? Do the cages appear crowded, or do the animals inside have some room to move around?

Did someone greet you when you walked into the store? Is the store staff friendly? Do they seem to care that you came in to shop? Remember that you will be visiting a pet store every week or two to purchase food, toys and other items for your pet, so you will want to select a store with friendly and knowledgeable people behind the counter.

After you've determined whether the store is clean and the employees are pleasant, find out if the staff tries to keep their birds in good health. Do they ask you to wash your hands with a mild disinfectant before handling their birds or between handling birds? If they do, don't balk at the request. This request is for the health of the birds, and it indicates that the store is concerned about keeping its livestock healthy. Buying a healthy bird is much easier and more enjoyable than purchasing a pet with health problems, so don't be afraid to follow the rules in a caring store!

If something about the store, staff and livestock doesn't feel quite right, choose another establishment with which to do business. If the store and its livestock meet with your approval (as they often will), then it's time to get down to the all important task of selecting your pet bird.

Look at the birds that are available for sale. If possible, sit down and watch them for awhile. Don't rush this important step. Do some of them seem bolder than the others? Consider those first because you want a curious, active, robust pet, rather than a shy animal that hides in a corner. Are other birds sitting off by themselves, seeming to sleep while their cagemates play? Reject any birds that seem too quiet or too sleepy because these attributes can indicate illness.

Here are some of the indicators of a healthy parrot. Keep them in mind when selecting your pet.

- bright eyes

- clean cere (the area above the bird's beak that covers its nares or nostrils)

- upright posture

- full-chested appearance

- actively moving around the cage

- clean legs and vent

- smooth feathers

- good appetite

Remember that healthy birds spend their time engaged in four main activities—eating, playing, sleeping and eliminating. If you notice that a bird seems to only want to sleep, for example, reject that bird in favor of another whose routine seems more balanced.

You may think that saving a small, picked-upon parrot from its cagemates seems like the right thing to do, but please resist this urge. Do not buy a bird because you feel sorry for it. You want a strong, healthy, spirited bird, rather than "the runt of the litter." Although it sounds hard-hearted, automatically reject any birds that are being bullied, are timid or that hide in a corner or shy away from you. It will save you some heartache in the end.

When you approached the parrots under consideration, did they hold their ground, or did they retreat into a safe corner of the cage? Did they take an interest in you, or did they shy away? Birds that hold their ground and take an interest in store visitors have better pet potential than those that flee or hide in a corner.

You can further test the pet potential of a parrot you're considering by putting your hand slowly up to the bird's cage or perch. If the bird stays where it is on the perch or cage or acts curious about your hand, it has better pet potential than if it scoots away from you or flies to the back of its cage.

If possible, let your new pet choose you. Many pet stores display their birds in colony situations on play gyms, or a breeder may bring out a clutch of babies for you to look at. If one bird waddles right up to you and wants to play, or if one comes over to check you out and just seems to want to come home with you, that's the bird you want!

One Bird or Two?

A question that some first-time bird owners who are considering smaller birds, such as budgies, cockatiels and lovebirds, ask is "Should I get one bird or two?" Single pet birds generally make more affectionate pets because you and your family become the bird's substitute flock. But a pair of birds can be quite entertaining as they chase each other around the cage and generally encourage each other into all sorts of avian mischief.

One small drawback of owning two pet budgies or cockatiels, especially young ones, is that they may have a tendency to playfully tug on one another's tail feathers. Sometimes these feathers come out, leaving you with two considerably shorter birds until the next set of tail feathers grows in.

If you have a pair of birds that suddenly become tailless, check the cage bottom for the feathers and watch your birds to see if they do, indeed, chase and pester each other. If not, you have nothing to worry about. If so, please alert your avian veterinarian to the problem and ask for further guidance. Two birds are also less likely to learn to talk because they can chatter to each other in their language rather than learning the language of their substitute "flock."

Let the size of your home, the size of the cage you have chosen and the amount of time you have to devote to your birds decide how many you will take home with you. Remember, two birds means more work than one, but they can also double your amusement and enjoyment of birds.

If you initially decide on a single pet bird and later add another, plan to house the birds in separate cages, at least at first. Introducing a new bird to another bird's cage opens up the possibility of territorial behavior on the part of the original bird. This territorial behavior can include bullying the newcomer and keeping it away from food and water dishes to the point that the new bird cannot eat or drink.

To avoid this problem, house the birds in separate cages until you can supervise their interactions. Let the birds out together on a neutral play gym and watch how they act with each other. If they seem to get along, you can move their cages closer together. Some birds will adjust to having other birds share their cages, while others prefer to remain alone in their cages with other birds close by.

Don't try to house a significantly larger or smaller bird with your existing pet because one or both of the birds could become injured during play or in a dispute over perches or food bowls. Moreover, certain small birds do not make good cagemates for other small birds of a different species. For example, budgies may tend to bully finches and canaries, keeping them away from food and water bowls, while cockatiels and lovebirds may exhibit the same behavior toward budgies.

To keep peace in your avian family, make sure every bird has its own cage, food and water bowls. Some birds will get along with other birds during supervised playtime on a play gym, while others do not "work and play well with others" and enjoy being the only pets out on the gym.

The Pre-owned Parrot

Many pet bird owners start with young, hand-fed birds, but some people adopt an adult parrot. You may be wondering which option is the right one, but there is no one right answer. If you have the time to devote to a hand-fed parrot's needs, then that should be the option you should explore. If you don't want to start with a young bird, then by all means you should look into adopting an adult parrot.

Keep in mind that adopting a young parrot may be less demanding because the bird hasn't had a chance to develop many bad habits. In some cases, bringing home an adult bird could be a great mistake (if the bird has a number of behavioral problems). On the other hand, it could be the best investment you'll ever make.

People put adult birds up for sale for many reasons. Perhaps the bird detects stress in the home and begins to pull its feathers, and the owners have neither the time nor the patience to solve the problem. The owners may have a child and suddenly no longer have time for the parrot, or they may be moving and cannot take their pet with them. Some people simply lose interest in their birds and sell them after a few years.

*Adopting a previously
owned parrot can provide
a bird owner with a great
deal of enjoyment, or it can
cause a lot of heartache.
Think carefully about
bringing home an adult
bird.* (PHOTO BY JULIE

My experience with a previously owned adult parrot has been completely sat-isfying, but it has required a considerable investment of time, patience and money to restore my African grey's health and allow her charming personality to come through. I can't guarantee that you'll find a diamond in the rough like I did when I adopted my adult bird, but I would certainly encourage you to consider an adult bird when you're looking for a pet.

If you do consider an adult bird, get as much background information as pos-sible from the bird's current owner. Has the bird been moved from home to home, or is the current owner the bird's first owner? Why is the bird being put up for adoption? Has the bird been seen by a veterinarian recently?

Examine the bird closely. Does the bird seem to have all its feathers? Does it scream the entire time you're visiting the current owner? Does it cower in the cor-ner of its cage? Does it seem to want to make your acquaintance, or does it seem uninterested in its surroundings?

Listen to what your heart and your head tell you when you see this bird. Don't adopt it because you feel sorry for it—you are bound to regret your deci-sion later. If you and the bird seem to have a bond, consider adopting it. If, how-ever, the bird shows all its problem behaviors in a single visit, look elsewhere for your chosen pet.

chapter 3

NORMAL PARROT BEHAVIORS

Parrots can display a wide range of personalities. Some parrots are naturally outgoing and enjoy showing off. They sing or do tricks for complete strangers. Others will talk for family members, while still others only talk for their favorite person in the home. Some parrots are real cuddlebugs, requiring regular

Some parrots enjoy cuddling, while others like to be admired from afar. (PHOTO BY PAMELA L. HIGDON)

sessions of cuddling and scratching, while others prefer to be admired from a distance. Some are playful, while others are reserved.

Regardless of the personality of the parrot you select as a pet, keep in mind that all parrots like routine. They seem to appreciate knowing that they will be fed about the same time every day, and that at other times of the day someone will take them out and pay attention to them, perhaps putting them on a play gym or maybe just cuddling them while watching television. Parrots also like to know that bedtime will occur at about the same time every night. As a result, you may find yourself with a little feathered alarm clock on your hands.

Parrots do not know the difference between workdays and weekends. Don't be surprised if your parrot wakes you at 7:30 on weekend mornings if that's the time it's accustomed to getting its morning round of attention and its breakfast.

Some parrots can be subtle about the way they wake you up. They may rustle lightly under their cage covers or bump into their toys quietly. Others take a more direct approach, talking or whistling or even yelling for attention until someone comes to uncover them.

Although they are creatures of habit, parrots can accept changes in their routines and schedules. You can vary your pet's routine a little bit, but you should be prepared to meet your pet's needs on a regular basis. Don't serve it breakfast at 6:30 on the weekdays and expect it to wait until 11 to eat on the weekends. After your bird has had some attention and you've served it breakfast, it will usually let you crawl back in bed for those last few precious minutes of weekend catch-up sleep.

To illustrate how much time a parrot requires, let me outline my morning schedule: I come downstairs and let Sindbad out of her cage. I remove her evening food and water bowls and hold her over the trash can so she can defecate.

While I'm waiting for her to take care of business, I pet her head, scratch her back and rub under her wings. Not only does she get attention this way, but it's also the perfect opportunity for me to check her over for lumps, bumps, scrapes, ingrown feathers, food that's stuck to her face and beak and anything else that seems out of the ordinary. On a good day, this routine takes about 20 minutes. If she is feeling neglected or in need of more attention than usual, it can take 30 minutes or more.

After Sindbad has relieved herself, I put her on top of her cage and make her breakfast. I chop her fruits and vegetables, add them to the Nutriberries and almonds I've already placed in her bowl and serve the meal to Sindbad. While I make my own breakfast and get ready for the day, she's left atop her cage to play for another 30 minutes or so.

In addition to her morning attention, Sindbad has come to expect attention during the day and in the evening, too. When I worked outside the home, I usually came home for lunch to give her some time out of her cage at midday, then

Sindbad falls over to attract attention when she believes that she is being ignored. (PHOTO BY JULIE RACH)

she expected more time out of her cage before dinner and as much attention as I would give her in the evenings. This could have been as simple as having her sit next to me while I read or watched television or as involved as an extensive cuddling session in which I helped her preen hard-to-reach feathers.

Now I work at home, and she's come to expect short bits of attention throughout the day, either by a visit from me or by a trip to my home office and "helping" me write. (She does this mostly by sitting on my desk, clicking her beak at pictures of African greys in my office and looking at me.) If she doesn't receive the expected attention, she falls over in her cage and taps lightly on the side of the cage to have me come rescue her. Since she only does this when I am in the same room with her but am not paying attention to her, I believe this is a learned behavior that resulted from earlier experiences in my home. When she first came to me, Sindbad would fall over because of a variety of physical ailments. She would tap on the side of the cage with her beak to alert me that there was a problem, and I would pick her up and fuss over her. I believe she enjoyed the attention greatly and knows how to receive more of it.

All in all, Sindbad gets a minimum of two hours of attention from me each day—and that's about as little as a parrot can stand.

Safe and Sound

Your parrot needs to feel secure. You can help it feel secure by providing it with a safe home in a large cage that is set up in a part of your house that is fairly active. In this way, your parrot feels as if it is part of your family or flock. By giving it a cage, you also give it a place where it can relax and just be a bird. Be sure this cage has at least one solid wall behind it. Being housed in the middle of a room may unduly stress your parrot because it may be on the lookout for surprise attacks from all sides of the cage.

Your bird may benefit from having a window near its cage, but make sure that your pet is not exposed to long periods of direct sunlight. (PHOTO BY JULIE RACH)

You can add variety to your bird's environment by putting its cage near a window. Be sure, however, not to place the cage completely in the window because your bird may overheat in the direct daylight. Parrots cannot sweat as mammals can, so owners have to be sure to protect their pets from temperature extremes.

The Empathetic Parrot

A parrot can read its owner's moods very well. If you're in a hurry and rushing around, don't be surprised if your bird's behavior takes a turn for the worse. If I try to rush my bird, she reacts by throwing miniature tantrums, becoming fussy and unhandleable.

When she first arrived in my home, my bird would show her displeasure with being rushed by biting me, and I still have the scars on my hands to show for my lack of judgment. Fortunately for my fingers, she has chosen to vocalize at me more than bite for the last five years, and I have learned to heed those vocalizations and slow down rather than get both of us excited over some minor stress. Interestingly, Sindbad has learned to express herself with increased moderation—the screams followed the biting period for about a year, and the screams have now been replaced with a series of squeaks, trills and other noises that are delivered with a variety of intonations.

Birds are very tuned in to their owner's moods. Some cockatiel owners who have epilepsy say that their birds can sense when their owners are about to have a seizure. (PHOTO BY JERRY THORNTON)

Common Conduct

The following common avian behaviors are listed, in alphabetical order, to help you better understand your new feathered friend!

Aggression

Parrots show aggression in many ways. They may click their beaks in a short series of clicks, raise one foot or raise their wings above their backs like little eagles ready to swoop down and attack. Aggressive birds may also signal their intentions by fanning their tails, pinning their eyes or wiping an already clean beak on a perch.

Other aggressive gestures include raising the nape and back feathers while keeping the head feathers low and crouching like a tightly coiled spring. The mouth is open and the bird is ready to strike if you are foolish enough to put your hand near. Some birds drum their wings to indicate that you are invading their space and an attack may be in the offing, while still others lean away from their cagetop or perch with beaks open to defend their space.

Attention-Getting Behaviors

As your parrot becomes more settled in your home, don't be surprised if you hear subtle little fluffs coming from under the cage cover in the morning. It's as if your bird is saying, "I hear that you're up. I'm up, too. Don't forget to uncover me and play with me!" Other attention-getting behaviors include gently shaking toys, sneezing or soft vocalizations. In addition to the early morning attention-getting behavior, some parrots will try to distract their owners when they are on the phone or have their attention otherwise diverted from the bird. In the case of my parrot, she acts up by vocalizing loudly while I'm on the phone, yet when I'm out of the room working or watching television in the same room as she is, she's a perfectly well-behaved bird.

Amazons and cockatoos may display for attention. They will throw their heads back, open their wings and fan their tails, almost as if they're demanding everyone in the room to look at them.

Some birds will beg to be petted by crouching low on their perches and holding their wings slightly away from their body. The begging bird will also stare at the neglectful offender. Extreme examples of attention-getting behavior include screaming and biting.

Bathing

In their natural habitats, birds bathe according to the opportunities presented to them. Some parrots, such as those that live in the canopy of the rain forest, bathe in rainfall. In captivity, these birds like showers or misting because it is similar to the rainfall to which their ancestors are accustomed.

Others bathe in puddles of water or by rolling around in wet grass. These birds will likely bathe in a shallow dish of water or by rolling in damp greens, including those in their food bowls.

Many birds seem to enjoy taking baths. You will have to experiment with your pet bird to see which type of bath it prefers. If you want to mist your pet, remember to use a spray bottle filled only with warm, clean water. Spray the water over the bird's head so that the mist falls on it like rain, rather than spraying the water directly into the parrot's face. Be sure the bottle itself hasn't held any chemicals because these could be harmful to your bird's health. Mark the bottle as a bird sprayer to ensure that other family members won't use it to fertilize plants or clean the windows.

Beak grinding is an activity that shows that a parrot is content. Owners often hear their pets grinding their beaks as the birds drift off to sleep at night.
(PHOTO BY JULIE RACH)

Beak Clicking

If your bird clicks a single click of its beak at you and pins its eyes but otherwise looks unthreatening, it is merely greeting you. If your bird clicks a series of short clicks with its beak and raises its foot at you, it is guarding its cage against attack, and the click is a warning for you to back off or the bird will attack you.

Beak Grinding

If you hear your bird making odd little grinding noises as it's drifting off to sleep, don't be alarmed! Beak grinding is a sign of a contented pet bird, and it's commonly heard as a bird settles in for the night. Some experts believe that this action helps a bird keep its lower beak in top condition for eating, and the bird grinds its beak at bedtime to be ready to eat again first thing in the morning.

Beak Wiping

After a meal, it's common for a parrot to wipe its beak against a perch or on the cage floor to clean it. Your pet will also wipe its beak on your arm or shirt, if they are within reach when its beak is dirty.

    If another bird is in the area, the bird that is wiping its beak is marking its territory. You will also see the territory-defending bird move toward the intruding parrot's feet with its beak. In some cases, the defender will chase the intruder off, while in others, the defender will decide to back off.

Burrowing

Some species, especially *Brotogeris,* macaws, conures and caiques, think it's great fun to burrow under their owners' clothing to play hide and seek. Conures will

Brotogeris, *such as this grey-cheeked parakeet, are happy to burrow under their owner's clothing.* (Photo by Gary A. Gallerstein, DVM)

also hide under their cage papers or cage covers if allowed to do so. If your bird likes to burrow, be careful that it doesn't get sat upon or squashed while playing. You may also want to wear a certain special "birdie outfit" for these play sessions because some birds also like to chew on their owners' clothing!

Chewing

Birds love to chew, and they do it quite well! The reasons behind chewing range from keeping a bird's beak in condition to burning off nervous energy. Whatever the reason, your bird will need a variety of chew toys to destroy in order to keep it happy and healthy. If a bird doesn't have chew toys, it may gnaw on its perches, the paper in its cage tray or other items that are not good for it to chew on— houseplants, door jambs, antique furniture or electrical cords.

If your bird is a chewer, be sure to check the finish on its cage to ensure that the finish is not chipped, bubbled or peeling because your pet may find the spot

If your bird likes to chew on its cage, make sure that it cannot injure itself by ingesting pieces of the cage finish. (PHOTO BY JULIE RACH)

and continue removing the finish, which, if ingested, can cause your bird to become ill. If you are considering a galvanized cage, be aware that some birds can become ill from ingesting pieces of the galvanized wire. You can prevent this "new cage syndrome" by washing down the cage wires thoroughly with a solution of vinegar and water, then scrubbing the cage with a wire brush to loosen any stray bits of galvanized wire. Rinse the cage thoroughly with water and allow it to dry before putting your bird into its new home.

Supervise your bird when it's out of its cage: A well-watched bird can't destroy the television remote. It can't chew through phone cords or electrical wires, and it can't nibble on houseplants, baseboards or furniture. Think of your bird as its own worst enemy in many cases because its natural curiosity can lead it into all sorts of temptation. As a conscientious bird owner, you want to protect your pet from all dangers, including itself and its curious nature.

Climbing

Parrots are agile creatures that often use their beaks as a third foot to help them get where they want to go. Chains, cage legs, lamp cords and curtain ropes are all liable to be climbed by your parrot in its quest to move from point A to point B.

Drinking

You will notice that your bird drinks water by scooping the water up in its lower beak, then tipping its head back to let the water run down its throat.

You will need to provide your parrot with fresh, clean drinking water to maintain its good health. Change the water at least twice a day, and more often if your bird has a tendency to drop food in its bowl or if it defecates in the bowl.

You can offer water to your bird in a shallow dish that clips onto the side of the cage, or you may find that a water bottle does the trick. If you are considering a water bottle, be aware that some clever parrots have been known to stuff a seed into the drinking tube, which allows all the water to drain out of the bottle. This creates a thirsty bird and a soggy cage, neither of which are ideal situations.

Note: If you would like to convert your bird from using a water dish to a water bottle, make sure it knows that the bottle contains water and how to use it before you stop offering the bird water in a bowl.

If you want to share a beverage with your bird, make sure that it has its own drinking vessel. Don't share caffeinated drinks, such as coffee or soda, and don't offer your pet alcohol. Neither caffeine's stimulant effects nor alcohol's sedating nature are good for your pet bird. Better choices for your pet are clean, fresh water or unsweetened fruit juice.

Eating

For your bird, eating is more than just filling its nutritional needs. An interesting array of fresh foods can help stimulate your bird's brain and make its daily routine a little more interesting. Offering your pet a balanced diet may also help it avoid behavioral problems, such as biting, screaming or chewing, and it may help increase the bird's playfulness and activity levels.

Some birds shred their food, which is a normal play behavior and shouldn't be a cause for concern. Others root through their food bowls rather abruptly, raking across the top of the food to find choice morsels. The food that gets tossed aside in the hunt for the extra-special goodies may be completely ignored, or your bird may give it a second look later in the day.

At the start of each meal, my parrot goes through her dish looking for almonds, which are currently her most favored food. Other favored foods in the past have included cheddar cheese, walnuts, apple slices or pomegranates. After she finds her favored food, she eats it, then goes back to select something else from the bowl. She tends to ignore any food that is thrown out of the bowl and ends up on the floor of her cage, but she will sort through the contents of the dish several times during the day to ensure that she hasn't missed anything. Sometimes I encourage her to go back for seconds or thirds by adding things to her dish throughout the day.

Birds generally eat only during daylight hours, although you may hear your pet rustling around under its cage cover to get a last bite or two of supper before it goes to sleep at night. Birds eat small quantities of food throughout the day to replenish their metabolisms, which is why many bird keepers provide a constant supply of food (seeds or pellets) to their pets at all times. Others prefer to feed their birds once in the morning and once in the evening. Whichever method suits you and your birds is fine.

I choose to have food available to my parrot at all times, day or night, and she has become accustomed to this. She has seeds and nuts available to her in the evening, and more seeds, nuts and fresh foods are offered during the day.

Parrots are social eaters, which means they may dive into their food bowls when they see you sit down to a meal. Your pet may also take an interest in whatever you are eating. Some parrots seem to think that the crackling sound your hand makes as it works down into a pretzel bag or the opening of a fresh bag of just-popped microwave popcorn is an open invitation for you to share whatever you're eating.

Sharing healthy people food with your parrot is completely acceptable, but sharing something that you've already taken a bite of is not. Human saliva contains bacteria that are perfectly normal for people but are potentially toxic to birds. For your bird's health and your peace of mind, always give your bird its own portion or plate.

There are certain foods that you should never give to your feathered friend. *Do not feed* rhubarb or avocado (the skin and the area around the pit can be toxic) to your pet. Don't give your parrot any foods that are highly salted, sweetened or fatty (such as pretzels, candy or potato chips). Chocolate contains theobromine, a chemical which birds cannot digest well. Simply put, chocolate can kill your parrot, so resist the temptation to share this snack with your pet. You will also want to avoid giving your bird seeds or pits from apples, apricots, cherries, peaches, pears and plums because they can be harmful to your pet's health.

Small parrots, such as budgies and lovebirds, can eat from the plastic dishes that come with their cages or from flat pie plates or the plastic dishes that many

Some foods can double as chew toys. Challenge your pet's mental faculties by offering it a variety of foods, some of which require a little work to enjoy. (PHOTO BY JULIE RACH)

frozen dinners come in (be sure to wash the dish thoroughly to remove all traces of your meal before reusing the dish for your pet). Larger parrots, such as greys, Amazons, conures and cockatoos, seem to enjoy food crocks, which are open ceramic bowls that allow them to hop up on the edge of the bowl and pick and choose what they will during the day. Crocks are also heavy enough to prevent mischievous birds from upending them, which can leave the bird hungry and the owner with quite a mess to clean up. You may also want to consider purchasing a cage with locking bowl holders because bowls that are locked in place (but are still easy to remove by bird owners at mealtime) are less likely to be upset by medium to large parrots.

Eye Pinning

When your bird sees something that excites it, frightens it or interests it greatly, its pupils will dilate, then contract, then dilate again. This behavior is known as eye pinning. Birds will pin their eyes when they see a favorite food, a favored person, another bird or a special toy. They will also pin their eyes when they are sexually excited, upset or aggressive. Eye pinning is described as "flashing" or "blazing" by some experts.

In larger parrots, eye pinning can also be a sign of confused emotions that can leave an owner vulnerable to a nasty bite. Watch your bird carefully if you see it pin its eyes. It could be greeting you warmly, or this could be an indication that the bird will bite soon!

Facial Feather Twitching

Cockatiels and cockatoos are prone to twitching their facial feathers. This gesture often occurs when the bird is startled or mildly irritated by something, although some birds do this when they are intrigued.

Eye pinning can indicate that a bird is very interested in something. Here, Sindbad pins at the prospect of a favorite treat—a slice of green apple. (PHOTO BY JULIE RACH)

Fluffing is a common parrot behavior that often precedes preening. (PHOTO BY JULIE RACH)

Fluffing

Fluffing is often a prelude to preening or a tension releaser. If your bird fluffs up, stays fluffed and resembles a little feathered pine cone, however, contact your avian veterinarian for an appointment because fluffed feathers can be an indicator of illness.

Flying in Place

Parrots with clipped wings sometimes exercise their wing and chest muscles by flying in place. These birds tightly grip their perch or the top of their cage and flap furiously for a few moments. The "flying" parrot will also hold onto a cage wall with its beak while flying in place.

Flying in place may indicate that a bird wants your attention. It can also mean that the bird is happy or that it is trying to tell you something important.

Foot Tapping

Cockatoos are most likely to demonstrate this behavior, although other species may do so. A bird that feels threatened in its space may tap its foot to establish its dominance over the area. It is often used as a bluff, but a bird may follow it up with other aggressive behaviors, so be cautious.

Hanging Upside Down

Some birds enjoy hanging upside down from the curtains, drapery rods or inside their cage. My bird used to do this quite often to demonstrate that she was content and at peace with her surroundings, but it caused the veterinarian's office staff a great deal of concern the first time they saw her do it. Hanging upside down is perfectly normal behavior for some birds, but this can be a bit unsettling if you aren't ready for it!

Head Shaking

Some cockatiels shake their heads when they hear particular noises or pitches. Experts disagree as to the meaning of this behavior—some believe that the bird is reacting negatively to the sound by shaking its head, while others argue that head shaking indicates that the bird is enjoying the sound.

Interacting with Their Owners

One of the simplest ways that parrots interact with their owners is to seek out some scratching. A bird with an itchy head will nudge its head under your hand until your fingers fall on the itchy spot, or it will approach you with its head down in a gesture of solicitation. If your parrot is molting when it comes to you seeking a scratch, pet it very gently because incoming feathers are often sensitive to the touch.

Parrots also like to interact with their owners during mealtime (pull a portable perch up to the table and let your bird join your family) or while the owner is watching television or reading (your bird can perch on the arm of your chair while you take part in these activities). Remember that parrots are social creatures that need interaction with other members of their flock, and in the home, you and your family are your bird's substitute flock.

Jealousy

Some birds become very possessive of their owners, and when they feel that they are not being given enough attention, they demonstrate their displeasure in a number of ways. These demonstrations can include tearing up their cages, nibbling on or biting their owners' hands, screaming or making other noises when their owners are on the phone.

To prevent your bird from becoming a problem pet, be sure to provide it the opportunity to entertain itself in its cage from time to time. Don't reward its screaming for attention (you'll soon learn which screams are just for the joy of making noise and which ones indicate a pet in danger or pain), and don't bribe your pet into silence with treats while you are out of the room or on the phone. If you do, your bird will soon have you wrapped around its wing feathers and will take full advantage of the situation.

Mobility

Most psittacine birds walk pigeon-toed and appear to waddle when they walk, while passerines and softbills hop from perch to perch. Birds kept in captivity should have their wings clipped to prevent them from flying into windows, mirrors and walls or escaping through an open door or window. Obviously, pet birds can be carried from place to place by their owners. Take care to keep the bird at chest level or slightly below to maintain control of your pet.

Mutual Preening

This part of the preening behavior, described later in this section, can take place between birds or between birds and their owners. Mutual preening can also be a way for birds to "kiss and make up" after a disagreement. Mutual preening is a gesture of affection reserved for best friends or mates, so consider it an honor if your bird wants to preen your eyebrows, hair, mustache or beard, or your arms and hands.

If your bird wants to be preened, it will approach you with its head down and will gently nudge its head under your hand as if to tell you exactly where it wants to be scratched and petted—usually in an area that the bird itself cannot reach, such as the top of its head or under its chin.

Napping

Don't be surprised if you catch your parrot taking a little catnap during the day. As long as you see no other indications of illness, such as a loss of appetite or a fluffed-up appearance, there is no need to worry if your pet sleeps during the day.

Pair Bonding

Pair bonding is usually discussed in the context of breeding; however, not only mated pairs bond. Best bird buddies of the same sex will demonstrate some pair bonding behavior, including sitting close to each other, preening each other and mimicking the other's actions, such as stretching or scratching.

As you watch a bonded pair, you will see that one bird is generally dominant and the other is submissive. The submissive bird will usually let its partner eat first and have the best spot on the perch.

Parrots need about 12 hours of sleep daily. They occasionally take short naps in the middle of the day.
(PHOTO BY JULIE RACH)

Perching

During the day, your parrot will alternate the feet on which it perches. It will draw one foot or the other up into its belly feathers to rest it. If you see your bird resting on one foot with its beak tucked into its back feathers, it's a happy bird that's about to take a nap.

If your bird perches on both feet all the time, it may be showing signs of illness, or it may be uncomfortable in its environment. If it sits low on its perch with its feathers fanned out over its feet, it's a happy bird that's keeping its feet warm. However, if your bird perches low on its perch and shows any signs of illness, such as labored breathing or watery eyes, contact your avian veterinarian immediately for an evaluation.

Picking Its Feet

Healthy parrots will groom their feet as part of their regular routine. Occasionally bits of food become stuck to a bird's feet, or small flakes of dead skin will need to be removed.

In certain cases, a bird can overgroom its feet, picking the skin until the foot bleeds. A small injury may be the cause of this behavior, but not all parrots that overgroom their feet have injured feet before the picking begins. If you see your parrot has become overly interested in grooming its feet, contact your avian veterinarian for an evaluation.

Playing

Playing is a vital part of a bird's life. Play gives parrots something to do physically and mentally with the energy they would expend in the wild while foraging for food. Playing helps fill the time when the birds' owners are unable to entertain them. It also helps a bird reduce frustration. Finally, playing simply lets birds have fun!

Some fun toys can be made at home. Offer your pet some raw pasta, nuts and bolts or an empty paper towel roll as a change of pace from its other toys. Make sure that nuts, bolts and other small items are clean and of a size that your pet can't swallow them. (PHOTO BY JULIE RACH)

Introduce new toys to your bird by setting them next to your pet's cage for a few days before putting them inside. (PHOTO BY JULIE RACH)

To help your bird play more productively, you will need to provide it with some toys. If your bird doesn't have any toys, it will make some by using its own feathers, dishes, food or other items within its cage.

Good choices for store-bought toys include sturdy wooden toys (either undyed or painted with bird-safe vegetable dye or food coloring) strung on closed-link chains or vegetable-tanned leather thongs, colorful toys that are made of parrot cookies, soft wooden blocks to encourage chewing and rope toys. If you purchase rope toys for your parrot, make sure its nails are trimmed regularly to prevent them from snagging in the rope, and discard the toy when it becomes frayed to prevent your bird from becoming tangled in the toy and accidentally injured.

Unsafe toys include brittle plastic toys that can be shattered easily by a parrot's strong beak, lead-weighted toys that can be cracked open to expose the dangerous lead to curious birds, loose link chains that can catch toenails or beaks and jingle-type bells that can trap toes, tongues or beaks.

Some entertaining toys can be made at home. Give your bird an empty paper towel roll or toilet paper tube (from unscented paper only, please), string some uncooked pasta on a piece of vegetable-tanned leather or offer your bird a dish of raw pasta pieces to destroy.

You might want to leave the toy next to the cage for a few days before actually putting it inside. Some birds accept new items in their cages almost immediately, but others need a few days to size up a new toy, dish or perch before sharing cage space with it.

Possessiveness

Some parrots can become overly attached to one person in the household, especially if that same person is the one who is primarily responsible for their care.

Indications of a possessive parrot can include hissing and other threatening gestures made toward other family members, and pair bonding behavior with the chosen family member.

You can keep your bird from becoming possessive by having all members of the family spend time with your bird from the moment you bring it home. Encourage different members of the family to feed the bird and clean its cage, and make sure all family members play with the bird and socialize with it while it's out of its cage.

Preening

Preening is part of a parrot's normal routine. You will see your bird ruffling and straightening its feathers each day. It will also take oil from the uropygial or preen gland at the base of its tail and put the oil on the rest of its feathers, so don't be concerned if you see your pet seeming to peck or bite at its tail. If, during

Birds with crests, such as cockatoos and cockatiels, appreciate a little help from their owners when it comes to preening the crest feathers. (Photo by Pamela L. Higdon)

Some birds display affection for their owners by preening their hair. (PHOTO BY PAMELA L. HIGDON)

Preening is another common parrot behavior. Pet birds spend a lot of time grooming their feathers during the course of the day. (PHOTO BY JULIE RACH)

molting, your bird seems to remove whole feathers, don't panic! Old, worn feathers are pushed out by incoming new ones, which makes the old feathers loose and easy to remove.

Regurgitating

If you see that your bird is pinning its eyes, bobbing its head and pumping its neck and crop muscles, it is about to regurgitate some food for you. Birds regurgitate to their mates during breeding season and to their young while raising chicks. It is a mark of great affection to have your bird regurgitate its dinner for you, so try not to be too disgusted should this occur.

Scratching

Budgies and cockatiels have remarkably flexible leg joints and are able to bring their legs up and behind their wings to scratch their heads. Larger parrots bring their heads and feet together in front of their bodies to execute a scratch.

Larger parrots may entice their owners to come over and pet them by slowly scratching their own heads, chins or necks while fluffing their head feathers.

Sensory Overload

If your bird suddenly pins its eyes, puffs its feathers up and seems to be a bundle of frenzied energy, look out! It has just gone into sensory overload, and it may bite you if you try to approach it under these conditions. If your bird acts like this, leave it alone until it calms down enough to be handled safely. Amazons seem quite prone to this behavior, but budgies and African greys are also subject to overstimulation.

Shyness Around Strangers

Some birds are reluctant to talk or perform around people who are unfamiliar to them. This is normal behavior, and if the bird has been exposed to new people and places properly by its owner, the bird will warm up to a new person rather quickly.

Side-Stepping

Side-stepping is a common movement frequently seen in budgies working their way across their cage on a perch. The bird scoots sideways along the perch and reaches its chosen destination rather quickly.

Sneezing

In pet birds, sneezes are classified as either nonproductive or productive. Nonproductive sneezes clear dust or a stray feather from a bird's nares (what we think of as nostrils) and are nothing to worry about. Some birds even stick a claw into their nares to induce a sneeze from time to time, much as a snuff dipper takes a pinch to produce the same effect. Productive sneezes, on the other hand, produce a discharge and are a cause for concern. If your bird sneezes frequently and you see a discharge from its nares or notice the area around its nares is wet, contact your avian veterinarian immediately to make an appointment.

Stress

Stress can show itself in many ways in your bird's behavior, including shaking, diarrhea, rapid breathing, wing and tail fanning, holding feathers tightly against the body, screaming, feather picking, poor sleeping habits or loss of appetite. The bird may also sit up tall on its perch and try to make itself appear as thin as possible.

Over a period of time, stress can harm your pet's health. To prevent your bird from becoming stressed, try to provide it with as regular a routine as possible.

Parrots are, for the most part, creatures of habit, and they don't always adapt well to sudden changes in their environment or schedule. If you do have to change something, talk to your parrot about it first. I know it seems crazy, but telling your bird what you're going to do before you do it may actually help reduce its stress.

Avian behaviorist Christine Davis advises owners to explain upcoming events to their birds. For example, I explain what I'm doing every time I rearrange the living room or when I have to leave my bird at the veterinarian's office for boarding during business trips. If you're going to be away on vacation, tell your bird how long you'll be gone, and count the days out on your fingers in front of the bird or show it a calendar.

Stretching

All parrots seem to engage in occasional bouts of stretching. An otherwise calm bird will suddenly grab the cage bars and stretch the wing and leg muscles on one side of its body, or it will raise both wings in imitation of an eagle. Again, this is normal behavior.

Tail Bobbing

If your bird's tail pumps or bobs when it's breathing, this is an indication of respiratory distress. However, it can also indicate exuberant vocalizing. If you see other signs of illness in conjunction with the tail bobbing, contact your avian veterinarian for an appointment.

Tail Flipping

Tail flipping is generally a sign that the bird is feeling happy. It seems to say, "Look at me, I am just on top of the world!" Or, as a parrot-owning friend of mine says, "You can just imagine a little thought bubble over their heads with the word 'Yahoo!' in it" when a bird flips its tail.

Tail Wagging

Birds that wag their tails may be expressing their happiness at seeing their owners, showing their interest in something or merely straightening their tail feathers. Tail wagging is often seen as part of an overall feather-fluffing greeting.

Tasting/Testing Things with the Beak

Birds use their beaks and mouths to explore their world in much the same way people use their hands. For example, don't be surprised if your bird reaches out to tentatively taste or bite your hand before stepping onto it the first time. Your bird isn't biting you to be mean; it's merely investigating its world and testing the strength of a new perch using the tools it has available.

Thrashing

African greys, some cockatoos and lutino cockatiels seem prone to a condition that is described as "night frights," "cockatiel thrashing syndrome" or "earthquake syndrome." Birds that experience thrashing episodes will be startled from sleep by loud noises or vibrations that cause a bird to awaken suddenly and try to take flight. In the case of caged pet birds, the thrasher may injure its wing tips, feet, chest or abdomen on toys or cage bars when it tries to flee from the perceived danger.

Bird owners can help protect their pets from harm by installing a small night-light near the bird's cage to help the bird see where it is during a thrashing episode, by placing an air cleaner in the bird's room to provide "white noise" that will drown out some potentially frightening background noises or by placing the bird in a small sleeping cage that is free of toys and other items that could harm a frightened bird.

Threats

If your bird wants to threaten a cagemate, another pet in the home or one of its human companions, it will stand as tall as it can and open its mouth. It will also try to bite the object of its threats.

Tongue Wiggling

When they see something they like very much, cockatiels and cockatoos open their beaks slightly and wiggle their tongues, then lick their beaks as if they've just eaten something tasty.

Vocalization

Many parrots vocalize around sunrise and sunset, which I believe hearkens back to flock behavior in the wild when parrots call to each other to start and end their days.

You may notice that your pet calls to you when you are out of the room. This may mean that it feels lonely or that it needs some reassurance from you. Tell it that it's fine and that it's being a good bird, and the bird should settle down and begin playing or eating. If it continues to call to you, however, you may want to check on it to ensure that everything is all right in its world.

If you hear your bird softly muttering to itself as it goes to sleep at night, chances are it is practicing talking. Listen to it carefully and see if you can deduce what it is trying to say. Many parrots practice their speech lessons quietly to themselves before trying their talking abilities on a larger audience.

Weak Legs

Some birds suddenly develop "weak legs" when they are put in their cages for time-out or at bedtime. A cockatoo I used to bird-sit was a master of this behavior, and it usually occurred when I was trying to put him up for the evening before he wanted to go to bed.

No matter how hard I tried to put him on his sleeping perch, his legs were too "weak" to support him and he had to stay on my hand until he felt up to the challenge of perching for the night. This routine usually lasted between five and ten minutes, and when he felt he had had adequate attention, he remembered how to perch in time to go to bed.

Wing Flipping

When birds are happy, they sometimes flip their wings to get their feathers just right. If they are preening, they may also flip their wings to get the feathers fluffed up so that they can be preened back in place. Note, however, that wing flipping can be tricky to interpret. It can mean that a bird is settling down to sleep, the bird is angry or the bird is in pain.

Wing Lifting

Birds often lift their wings to stretch them. They also lift their wings when they are warm in order to equalize their body temperatures. Birds have no sweat glands, so they must pant and lift their wings to remove excess heat from their bodies.

Yawning

You may notice your pet yawning from time to time or seeming to want to pop its ears by opening its mouth wide and closing it. Some bird experts would say your bird needs more oxygen in its environment and would recommend airing out your bird room (be sure all your window and door screens are secure before opening a window or sliding glass door to let fresh air in), while other experts would tell you your pet is merely yawning or stretching its muscles. If you see no other signs of illness, such as forceful regurgitation or vomiting, yawning, is no cause for concern.

This is *My* Space!

When visiting bird stores and the pet birds of friends, be aware that birds are territorial—this is a normal bird behavior. Don't poke your fingers into cages that hold a bird you do not know well. The bird will take this gesture as a threat, and will probably bite you for invading its space.

Be wary of strange birds, particularly larger parrots such as Amazons, cockatoos and macaws. Birds that do not know you may perceive you as a threat and may bite. At best, these bites pinch a finger and hurt a lot; at worst, you can end up like a customer at a pet store in Orange County, California, who required plastic surgery on her ear after being bitten by the store's scarlet macaw.

Species-Specific Behaviors

In addition to the common parrot behaviors described above, some behaviors are species specific.

African Greys

Like many parrots, African greys can see detail and discern colors. Unlike many parrots, greys can be highly sensitive to changes in their food dishes and other cage accessories and may refuse to eat. Be aware of this when selecting cage accessories for your pet. Some seem excited by a different colored bowl, while others act fearful of the new item. My African grey recognizes her black food trays and her red, blue, brown or ivory water bowls, but if I offer her food or water in a different color tray or bowl, she is hesitant to eat or drink right away. She must become accustomed to the new food vessel before she will use it, a process that can take as little as a few minutes or as long as half a day.

Some wild-caught greys have refused to eat from a bowl if it was a different color than the bowls to which they were accustomed, while others would eat only if the person feeding them wore the same clothes each day at feeding time.

African greys are clumsy, particularly when they are chicks. Make your grey feel more comfortable when you hold it or carry it by allowing it to rest its beak on your chest as it perches on your hand. Many birds feel more secure when they are held or carried in this manner.

Amazons

Amazons may beak fence with one another, which is a prelude to mating. In this gesture, two birds face off and try to grab the other's beak. If one bird manages to grab hold of the other's beak, the caught bird needs to only cry out a little, then the grabbing bird lets go. The birds then preen each other, followed by more fencing.

Amazons may also demonstrate their excitement by blowing and snorting air through their nares. An excited Amazon may crouch low on its perch, pin its eyes, hold its wings away from its body and snort. Owners of Amazons may notice that their birds' eyes rapidly dilate and contract when the bird is excited, frightened or pleased. The birds will also fan their tail feathers and fluff their neck feathers under these circumstances in order to look larger and more intimidating. To prevent yourself from being nipped severely, keep your hands away from any parrot that is pinning its eyes and fluffing its feathers. The bird could feel it needs to defend itself from a perceived threat (you, whether you're threatening or not) and will respond by biting or striking at you.

At around 3 or 4 years of age, yellow-naped Amazons have a tendency to become extremely possessive of their owners during breeding season. I saw two different yellow nape owners get bitten severely by the other person's bird during breeding season one year. In each case, the bird perceived the other person as a threat to his owner, and the bird chased off the intruder. Usually, yellow napes are really just interested in their owners and will bite them as punishment for daring to have interests unrelated to the bird itself.

Budgies

Be sure to offer only uncovered dishes to your budgie because many budgies would rather starve to death than eat out of a hooded or covered feeder.

When you're feeding your budgie, check the dish daily to ensure your bird has enough food. Because they are such neat eaters and drop the used hulls right back in their dishes, they can often fool you into thinking that they haven't finished their meal. Don't just look in the dish, but actually remove it from the cage and blow lightly into the dish (you might want to do this over the kitchen sink or the trash can) to remove seed hulls.

Cockatiels and Cockatoos

Cockatiels and cockatoos can say a lot with their crests, and observant owners can quickly learn how to read their pets' moods. Here's what to look for:

- Content birds keep their crests lowered. Only the tips of the feathers point upward.

- Playful, alert birds raise their crests vertically. This position indicates that the bird is ready for action.

- Agitated birds raise their crests straight up and have the feather tips leaning forward slightly.

- Frightened birds whip their crests back and hiss in a threatening manner. They also stand tall, ready to fight or flee as the situation dictates.

- Male cockatiels declare their love for their mates (or their owners) by raising their wings sideways after the wings are fully extended. The male cockatiel also bows his head and may dip his whole body forward as part of this courtship ritual.

Conures

Conures have several interesting behaviors, one of which is snuggling under something when they sleep. Don't be surprised to find your bird under a corner of its cage paper if the cage it lives in doesn't have a grille to keep the bird out of the cage tray. You can provide your conure with a washcloth, a fuzzy toy or something else cuddly to snuggle with.

Conures also fall asleep in their food bowls, often on their backs with their feet in the air. This seems to be an awkward or uncomfortable position to bird owners, and upon first encountering this behavior some owners have panicked, fearing that their pet has died. Despite its alarming first impression, there's nothing wrong with your conure if it naps on its back. Some parent birds even feed their chicks when the chicks are lying on their backs, and this is a perfectly comfortable position for a conure.

Conures are also great bathers, and they'll try to bathe in their water bowls if nothing else is available. Conures really prefer a dunking under the water faucet or to stand under a light shower in the kitchen sink. Be sure the water is lukewarm before letting your conure take a quick dip, and allow plenty of time for your bird's feathers to dry before it goes to bed (a blow-dryer set on low can accelerate the drying process).

Austral and slender-billed conures like to forage on cage bottoms for roots, tubers, leaf buds, seeds, nuts and fruits. Although bird owners are generally cautioned to be concerned if their birds seem to always be on the cage bottom, for these two conure species, it's perfectly natural behavior.

Eclectus

Female eclectus are conditioned to protect the food supply at all costs to ensure the survival of the species. When Rosebud, a female eclectus I have known since she was hatched in southern California about five years ago, gets defensive of her food bowls, she hovers in a "zone" near the bowls. Her owners cannot get her out of the zone and someone will get bitten if they remain in the area. Rosebud's owner has stopped handling any of her dishes when the bird is near.

Rosebud is so defensive that she recently "attacked" when her owner was washing another parrot's dishes, which look completely different from Rosebud's.

Female eclectus are notorious for attacking bare toes. If you have a female eclectus and allow her to roam free on the floor in your home, make sure that you wear shoes or prepare to be bitten. (PHOTO BY PAMELA L. HIGDON)

Rosebud's eyes turned a pale yellow, and she clamped down on her owner's finger and would not let go. The owner had to press on the skin that connects upper and lower mandibles. Because her owner knows that this is an instinctive behavior on the part of her pet bird, she has to simply leave Rosebud in her cage whenever she's preparing food—or suffer the consequences. Trying to punish the bird or alter this behavior is a lost cause.

The Young Parrot

Parrot chicks spend most of their time eating and sleeping. As they grow and mature, they go through developmental stages—their feathers grow, they develop motor and flight skills and become increasingly self-sufficient. Young parrots will also stretch their wings and scratch themselves in an effort to be more comfortable.

Owners of hand-raised chicks may notice that their birds will go through an "independent" phase in which the chicks move from being cute and dependent upon their owners to exploring their world. The birds will need a combination of nurturing to encourage them to explore and discipline to protect them from their curious natures.

It's up to you, the owner, to nurture and discipline your young parrot and to continue to do so throughout its lifetime. It is important to discipline your parrot, but discipline should be clearly distinguished from punishment. Parrots don't understand and therefore do not respond fruitfully to most forms of punishment

Young birds need guidance from their owners to ensure that they will be good pets. (PHOTO BY GARY A. GALLERSTEIN, DVM)

used by pet owners. Traditional forms of punishment often frighten, harm or anger parrots rather than achieve your desired result of getting them to behave better. "Time-outs" and other discipline methods used with children who are just starting school are very effective with most parrots. Withholding attention briefly or otherwise denying them a pleasure, such as a cuddle or a head scratch, will do more to encourage your parrot to behave than traditional forms of punishment.

The Mature Bird

When birds are between 2 and 5 years old, they reach sexual maturity. This stage of development brings with it another set of behaviors, many of which coincide with breeding season. These can include biting, screaming or striking at an owner who puts his or her hand into a bird's cage to change food or water bowls. Note that these actions are normal parrot behaviors. Once your parrot reaches sexual maturity, its hormonal drives during breeding season will largely determine its conduct. Unfortunately, you are not a parrot, so you may not see these behaviors as normal. They are, and they will pass. You may need to alter your behavior somewhat during breeding season to ensure that you get through it with flying colors.

Just as dogs or cats can be altered, so can pet birds. However, this surgery is not routinely recommended. It's a far riskier procedure for birds than for other pets, and it's not necessary in most cases. A veterinarian *might* recommend that you spay your female bird is if it is a chronic egg layer and other methods of treating the problem, such as hormone shots, have failed.

Senior Parrots

As your parrot grows older, you may notice some changes in its behavior and some subtle changes in its appearance and habits. It may molt more erratically and its feathers may grow in more sparsely as it ages, or it may seem to preen itself less often. You will need to pay more attention to your older bird's behavior and its routine because changes in its behavior may indicate illness.

Although little is known about the nutritional requirements of older pet birds, avian veterinarians Branson W. Ritchie and Greg J. Harrison suggest in their book *Avian Medicine: Principles and Applications* (coauthored with Linda R. Harrison) that older pet birds should eat a highly digestible diet, allowing it to maintain its weight while receiving lower levels of proteins, phosphorus and sodium. They also suggest that this diet contain slightly higher levels of vitamins A, B12, E, thiamin, pyridoxine, zinc, linoleic acid and lysine to help birds cope with the metabolic and digestive changes that come with old age.

Older pet birds are prone to a number of health problems, including tumors, vision problems, thyroid gland insufficiencies, chlamydiosis and upper respiratory infections.

If you notice that your pet's breastbone sticks out a little more than it used to or that your bird has difficulty perching, schedule an evaluation with your avian veterinarian. Both of these signs indicate possible tumor development. Tumors develop in pet birds most frequently in the nerves off the bird's spine. A tumor in this spot can impair kidney and gonad function, which can put pressure on the nerve that runs into the bird's leg.

Vision problems can show themselves in several ways. Your pet may no longer be able to judge distances well, or its eyes may appear clouded over. Just as in older people, cataracts can appear in older birds, especially budgies and macaws.

Thyroid problems occur frequently in older parrots, and are usually a result of either a deficiency in the bird's hormonal system or a need for supplemental iodine in the diet. If your bird suddenly gains weight and develops fat deposits that resemble tumors, contact your avian veterinarian to have your pet examined.

Although they may not seem to be connected, a thyroid problem may show itself in a longer-than-average molt. If you notice that your bird's molting period seems unusually long as it ages, talk to your avian veterinarian. A hormonal supplement may be in order to help keep your bird healthy.

You may need to pay more attention to the temperature of your bird's room as it grows older. Add supplemental heat by using an incandescent bulb covered with a reflector on one end of your bird's cage. This allows a bird to move closer to the heat source if it is cold and away from it if the bird becomes too warm. Make sure that the bulb is sufficiently far from the cage so that your pet cannot burn itself on the reflector or the bulb.

Notes from the Experts

These tips for successful bird ownership are found in avian behaviorist Christine Davis's behavior chapter in *The Complete Bird Owner's Handbook* by Gary A. Gallerstein, DVM:

1. **Offer variety in your bird's life:** Provide different toys and different locations in the home for your bird. If the bird starts to become noisy or rowdy, gently and lovingly return it to its cage for a little "time-out" of about 20 minutes. In this manner, your bird can rest, eat, have a drink of water or defecate. After it has had an opportunity to calm down, it can be returned to the location it was in when it started to act up.

2. **Anticipate and avoid potential problems:** Play with your bird or talk to it before it misbehaves to attract your attention. Make a fuss over it every few minutes, be sure to greet it every time you enter its room and say good bye to it when you leave. I tell my parrot that I'll be upstairs working when I leave her room, and she's quite content to stay on her cage floor, playing or eating. If she feels neglected, she calls to me quietly, or if she gets herself into a jam by knocking over her water bowl or getting caught in a corner she can't climb out of, she makes a somewhat bigger fuss to attract my attention. I go down and rescue her, then things return to normal.

3. **Don't reward undesirable behaviors:** Don't pay attention to your bird when it misbehaves—don't pick it up, don't look at it, don't talk to it and most certainly don't yell at it. Birds have a strong sense of drama, and they like all the commotion provided by being yelled at for misbehaving. If you react to your bird's misbehavior in any of these ways, the bird will feel rewarded and will misbehave again just to see you go through the motions of getting excited. Very soon, you will be well trained, and you will think that you have an impossible parrot on your hands.

4. **Respect your bird's intelligence:** Treat your parrot as an intelligent creature and it will behave better than if you treat it as "a dumb animal."

5. **Socialize your bird from an early age:** Play games with your parrot as soon as you bring it home, and give it consistent (but not constant) attention. Give it interesting toys to play with when you aren't available, and change these toys often. Show it different places in your house and introduce it to other family members so that it will not become dependent on one person in the family.

6. **Understand your pet's fears:** If your bird fears something new in its environment, take the time to help it overcome the fear. If the bird isn't sure about a new toy, for example, leave the toy out where the bird can see it for a few days and become adjusted to it before you put the toy in your bird's cage. You may even have to play with the toy yourself where your bird can see you to show your pet that there's nothing to fear from a new toy. In some cases, you may even have to put the toy away for a while and reintroduce it later, but your patience will pay off!

7. **Talk to your bird:** Look your bird in the eye and speak to it in a pleasant, animated voice. This is the way birds talk to each other in the wild, and you may notice that your bird talks back, either in human words or in little chirrups or feather fluffs.

Davis also outlines how to create the proper pecking order in your home flock, which will be critical to a happy coexistence with your pet.

Keep your bird off your shoulder—hold it and carry it at chest level. Birds consider you an equal if they can look you in the eye, and they may also consider the rest of your body a perch/tree. If something threatening comes along, your bird may bite at your face to encourage you to flee a frightening situation.

Letting a medium to large parrot sit on your shoulder results in a bird that is full of itself and hard to handle. By holding your bird at the level of your heart, you may also help soothe it because it can hear your heartbeat.

Avian behaviorist Sally Blanchard cites additional reasons for keeping your bird off your shoulder. In this position, it's difficult to maintain eye contact with your parrot, which makes it difficult to maintain control of your bird. Moreover, a bird on its owner's shoulder feels dominant because its eye level is above that of its owner.

In addition to these potential problems, parrots on shoulders may entertain themselves by nibbling on their owners' jewelry, pulling their hair or investigating their moles. None of these are desirable activities, and many can lead to injury for either the bird or the owner.

So what do you do if your bird is used to being on your shoulder? Begin training it to perch on your knee when you're watching television or to sit on the arm of your chair. If your bird tries to climb up to your shoulder, place your hand in front of your bird and tell it to step up, then place the bird back where you want it to sit. Eventually, your bird will get the idea that your shoulder is now off limits.

If you remember to keep your arm bent at the elbow and tucked in close to your ribcage, your bird will not have a ready-made ramp (your arm) to run up from your hand to your shoulder. This will also help discourage a former shoulder sitter from regaining its position of power.

Avian behaviorist Mattie Sue Athan believes that training plays a part in creating and maintaining good behavior in pet parrots, but she also cites certain environmental factors that can be manipulated to improve a bird's behavior. These factors are height, cage size, territory, location, light, accessories and access to appropriate choices, and she explains them completely in her book, *Guide to a Well-Behaved Parrot.*

In the home, Athan says height can be used to maintain good behavior in a parrot because parrots cooperate with those they have to look up to and they threaten anything they can look down on. If your parrot consistently perches at

Birds that sit on their owner's shoulders are likely to find jewelry an interesting chew toy.
(PHOTO BY JERRY THORNTON)

your eye level or above, it will be more difficult to handle than if you keep it at chest or waist level when it's out of its cage.

Athan believes that a bird needs a spacious cage in which to live, and that space should measure 1.5 times the bird's untrimmed wing span in at least two of the three dimensions (height, width, length).

Parrots that spend too much time in any one place can become aggressive or territorial, according to Athan. To combat this, an owner should provide perching places throughout the house away from the bird's cage. This helps replicate the wild environment in which parrots forage in several locations during the course of a day.

Location can be used to influence a parrot's behavior negatively when the bird is put into "solitary confinement" and isolated from the rest of the family, either literally or figuratively. The concept can be used positively when the bird is made to feel a part of family activities. Don't put your bird smack in the middle of the daily rush, though, because this can also lead to behavior problems resulting from the stress the bird feels by being at the center of what must seem like a ongoing hurricane.

Birds need exposure to light in order to maintain good health. If a parrot receives too little or too much light, it will experience physical and behavioral problems. Ensure that your bird receives adequate light, but don't overdo it.

Accessories are toys that the bird can play with, chew on, beat up and otherwise expend energy on, according to Athan. She recommends that parrots have about a half-dozen toys, and that some of them be used as rewards for good behavior.

The final factor—access to appropriate choices—means that the bird has many chances to behave well and few chances to misbehave. If a bird has an interesting environment in its cage or on its play gym—good food and safe toys that the bird likes to play with, for example—and if it is supervised while outside its cage, chances are that it will leave your belongings alone. If, however, you turn the bird loose with no guidance and provide it with nothing to play with, you may soon find it peeling the wallpaper off your walls or reducing your favorite wicker basket to splinters.

To avoid possible problems associated with having your bird sit on your shoulder, encourage it instead to sit on the arm of your chair as you watch television or read. (PHOTO BY PAMELA L. HIGDON)

chapter 4

BEHAVIORS THAT INDICATE ILLNESS

Despite their reputations as delicate pets, many parrots are really quite hardy if given proper daily care and attention. From time to time, however, your parrot may fall ill, and it's up to you to see that it gets proper veterinary care in order to make a full recovery. Avian veterinarian Gary Gallerstein lists the following signs of illness in parrots in his book, *The Complete Bird Owner's Handbook:*

- Changes in activity such as singing or talking less, sleeping more or decreased responsiveness to various stimuli.

- Changes in appearance such as ruffled feathers, weakness, an inability to perch, remaining on the cage floor, bleeding, injuries, convulsions or a distended abdomen.

- Breathing problems such as noisy breathing (wheezing, panting or clicking), heavy breathing (shortness of breath, open-mouthed breathing, tail bobbing), nasal discharge or swollen area around the bird's eyes or loss of voice.

- Digestive problems such as vomiting and/or regurgitation, diarrhea (it may include blood, mucus or whole seeds) or straining to eliminate.

- Changes in the bird's droppings in terms of number, consistency or color.

- Musculoskeletal problems such as lameness, drooping wings or a change in posture.

- Eye problems including swollen or pasted-shut eyelids, increased blinking, eye discharge, eyeball cloudiness, squinting or rubbing of the eye or the side of the face.

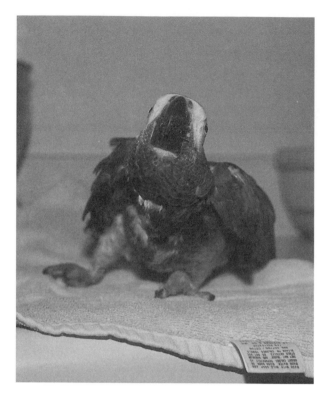

If you suddenly notice that your bird is favoring one leg, it could indicate illness or injury. (PHOTO BY JULIE RACH)

- Skin problems including lumps, bumps, excessive flaking of skin or beak, or overgrown beak or nails.

- Feather problems such as a prolonged molt, picking at or chewing feathers or damaged (broken, crushed, twisted or deformed) feathers.

- Changes in food or water intake including a loss of appetite, a loss of weight, dehydration, or a decrease or increase in food and water consumption.

If your bird shows any of these signs, please contact your veterinarian's office immediately for further instructions. Your bird should be seen as soon as possible to rule out any illnesses.

Feather Picking

As noted above, feather picking is a common avian behavior that could indicate illness. Feather picking is an extreme form of grooming in which a parrot not only preens its feathers, but picks at or pulls them.

Feather picking may have physical causes, such as a dietary imbalance, a hormonal change, a thyroid problem or an infection of the skin or feathers. It can also

Feather picking can be caused by illness, such as a Giardia *infestation. If your bird begins picking its feathers, have it evaluated by an avian veterinarian to rule out physical causes for the picking.* (PHOTO BY JULIE RACH)

result from a bird breaking a feather while it is a clumsy youngster. The feather hurts, so the bird picks at it to remove the source of the pain. If the bird has difficulty removing the feather, it may come to believe that picking helps alleviate pain. Be sure to check your bird's feathers regularly, and remove any broken feathers promptly. Ask your avian veterinarian for information on how to remove a broken feather.

Feather picking can also be caused by an emotional upset, such as a change in the owner's appearance, a change in the bird's routine, another pet being added to the home, a new baby in the home or a number of other factors.

Once feather picking begins, it may be difficult to get a bird to stop. Although it looks painful to us, some birds find the routine of pulling out their feathers emotionally soothing. Birds that suddenly begin picking their feathers, especially those under the wings, may have an intestinal parasite called *Giardia*. If you notice that your bird suddenly starts pulling its feathers out, contact your avian veterinarian for an evaluation.

Be aware that your bird may be quite discreet in showing signs of illness. Its routine may change subtly: It may just sleep a little more in the afternoon, or it may eat a little less. You don't really see a drastic change in its routine, but something just feels different. Experience has taught me to listen to those feelings. It's up to you as the bird's owner to be alert to any changes in your bird's routine and to bring these changes to the attention of your avian veterinarian.

In the wild, birds are masters of hiding illness or weakness because to demonstrate ill health makes the bird an easy target for predators. As a result, by the time many parrots show obvious signs of illness, they are really quite ill and they may not be able to be nursed back to health.

Common Avian Health Conditions

Aspergillosis

Aspergillosis is caused by a fungus, *Aspergillus*. It can settle in a bird's respiratory tract and cause breathing difficulties. This disease was once considered untreatable, but the use of antifungal medications from medicine designed for humans have brought some hope for a remedy.

Bumblefoot

Bumblefoot is an infection of the sole of the bird's foot. It can cause redness and inflammation, swelling and lameness. Antibiotics, bandages and surgery may be needed to treat the condition, which can be prevented by keeping a bird's cage clean and feeding it a well-balanced diet.

Candida

Candida is a disease caused by the yeast *Candida albicans*. Young birds seem to be particularly susceptible to candida infestations, which occur when a bird's diet is low in vitamin A. Signs of candida include white cheesy growths in the bird's mouth and throat, a loss of appetite, regurgitation or vomiting and a crop that is slow to empty.

Many adult birds show no signs of this condition, and therefore diagnosis is problematic. A breeder may not even know he or she has infected birds until the parent birds pass the yeast to the chicks during feeding. Even hand-fed chicks are not immune to the condition because they can be affected by it if their throats are damaged by feeding tubes. Veterinary assistance in the form of antifungal drugs and a diet high in vitamin A may be your best weapons against candida.

Giardia

Giardia is caused by a protozoan called *Giardia psittaci*. Signs of a *Giardia* infection include loose droppings, weight loss, feather picking (especially under the wings), loss of appetite and depression. Because the *Giardia* organism is difficult to detect in a bird's feces, a proper diagnosis may be very time-consuming. The disease can be spread through contaminated food or water, and birds do not develop an immunity to it. Your veterinarian can recommend an appropriate medication to treat *Giardia.*

Goiter

Goiter is an enlargement of the thyroid gland in a bird's throat. It is caused by an iodine deficiency and is most often seen in budgies that eat seed-only diets. Symptoms include difficulty in breathing and swallowing and regurgitation. Your veterinarian can determine if your budgie has a goiter through x-rays and blood tests. Iodine supplements are used to treat the condition.

Gout

Gout can be associated with kidney problems. Specifically, gouty birds have kidneys that are unable to remove excess nitrogen from the bird's bloodstream. This causes uric acid and urates to build up in the bird's body or in its joints.

The exact cause of gout is unclear at this time, but high levels of dietary sodium or calcium and inadequate fluid intake, may contribute to gout. Two forms of gout occur: articular gout, which affects a bird's lower leg joints as shiny, cream-colored swellings, and visceral gout, which affects a bird's internal organs and is difficult to diagnose. Articular gout is a painful condition that causes an affected bird to go lame.

Presently, no cure exists for gout, but treatment includes lowering protein levels and increasing the amount of fruits and vegetables in the bird's diet, along with treating any underlying infections that may have an impact on kidney function. Veterinarians may be able to lower a bird's uric acid levels with medication, and they can also prescribe drugs to ease the bird's pain. Padded perches also seem to offer comfort to afflicted birds.

This budgie is obese. It's a good idea for owners to weigh their birds regularly and to chart their weights. Always use a gram scale to weigh your bird, as it is considerably more accurate for our feathered friends than a traditional scale. (PHOTO BY GARY A. GALLERSTEIN, DVM)

Obesity

Obesity may be caused by a malfunctioning thyroid gland, but it is most often caused by a bird eating far more calories than it burns in a day. To prevent this from happening to your pet bird (particularly your budgie, Amazon or cockatoo), make sure that it eats a well-balanced diet that is low in oil seeds and nuts (sunflower seeds, millet, peanuts, walnuts) and that it receives ample opportunity to exercise both inside its cage and outside of it during supervised "out times" on a play gym.

If your bird is overweight, you may notice that it has developed a fatty growth, or lipoma, that may impair its ability to fly. Some experts think that these lipomas are linked to a lack of exercise in pet birds. The good news is that most lipomas can be removed safely by your veterinarian.

Papillomas

Papillomas are benign tumors that can appear almost anywhere on a bird's skin, including its foot, leg, eyelid or preen gland. If a bird has a papilloma on its

To encourage your parrot to exercise, you can place its food atop its cage so that the bird has to climb up to dine. (PHOTO BY JULIE RACH)

THE IMPORTANCE OF QUARANTINE

You can protect your pets against polyomavirus and other diseases. Quarantine new stock, shower and change your clothes before handling your pet when you've gone to other bird owners' homes, to bird marts that have large numbers of birds from different vendors on display or to bird specialty stores with unhealthy stock.

---

cloaca, the bird may appear to have a "wet raspberry" coming out of its vent. These tumors, which are caused by a virus, can appear as small, crusty lesions, or they may be raised growths that have a bumpy texture or small projections.

Many papillomas can be left untreated without harm to the bird, but if a bird picks at the growth and causes it to bleed, removal will be necessary.

Polyomavirus

Polyomavirus, which is sometimes called French moult, causes flight and tail feathers to develop improperly or not develop at all. Polyomavirus can be spread through contact with new birds, as well as from feather and fecal dust. Adult birds can carry polyomavirus but not show any signs of the disease. These seemingly healthy birds can pass the virus to young birds that have never been exposed, and these young birds can die from polyomavirus rather quickly.

Sick birds can become weak, lose their appetites, bleed beneath the skin, have enlarged abdomens, become paralyzed, regurgitate and have diarrhea. Some birds with polyomavirus suddenly die. At present, there is no cure, although a vaccine is under development.

Proventricular Dilatation Syndrome

Proventricular dilatation syndrome, formerly known as macaw wasting disease, is a serious disease of a bird's digestive system. Affected birds are unable to digest their food properly. Signs of proventricular dilatation syndrome include regurgitation, undigested food in the bird's droppings, diarrhea and severe weight loss. This disease is fatal, and no cure exists at present.

Psittacine Beak and Feather Disease Syndrome

Psittacine beak and feather disease syndrome (PBFDS) is caused by a virus first detected in cockatoos and was originally thought to be a cockatoo-specific problem. It has since been determined that more than 40 species of parrots can contract this disease, which causes a bird's feathers to become pinched or clubbed in appearance. Other symptoms include beak fractures and mouth ulcers. This highly contagious, fatal disease is most common in birds less than 3 years of age, and there is no cure.

Psittacosis

Psittacosis (also known as chlamydiosis or parrot fever) is a disease that some birds carry all of their lives, although symptoms may not surface for many years. Signs of the disease include nasal discharge, diarrhea, lime-green droppings, a loss of appetite, weight loss and depression. Some afflicted birds simply suffer a sudden death. Birds with psittacosis can be treated with tetracycline-laced pellets. Parrots can transmit this disease to people, and individuals with suppressed immune systems are particularly susceptible. However, transmission to humans is quite rare. Affected people display flu-like symptoms and should seek antibiotic treatment from their physicians.

Roundworms

Roundworms, or ascarids, can infest birds that have access to dirt, which is where roundworm eggs are found. The worms themselves are 2 to 5 inches long and resemble white spaghetti. Minor infestations of roundworms can cause weight loss, appetite loss, growth abnormalities and diarrhea, while heavy infestations can result in bowel blockage and death. To diagnose roundworms, your veterinarian will analyze a sample of your bird's droppings. He or she can then prescribe an appropriate course of treatment to alleviate the problem.

Sarcocystis

Sarcocystis, another parasite, can be a problem in North American areas with large opossum populations. Sarcocystis infections seem to be more prevalent in the winter months, and male birds seem more susceptible to this parasite than females. Birds affected by sarcocystis often appear healthy one day and are dead the next. Those birds that do show signs of illness before dying become lethargic, cannot breathe easily and pass yellowish droppings. Preventing opossums from gaining access to your aviaries can eliminate the threat of this disease. However, cockroaches can also pass along this parasite by consuming opossum feces and then being eaten by an aviary bird.

Scaly Face

Scaly face is a condition caused by the *Knemidokoptes* mite, which burrows into the top layers of a bird's skin around its cere, eyelids, vent or legs. This burrowing leaves white crusts on the bird's cere or the corners of the mouth.

  If allowed to progress, scaly face can cause lesions to develop on a bird's beak, eyelids, throat, vent, legs and feet. Advanced cases can also cause beak deformation and horny appendages on a bird's face and legs. The appendages can interfere with a bird's ability to move its legs and toes. If your avian veterinarian

Stress bars on your bird's feathers are an indication that something is not quite right in your parrot's environment. (PHOTO BY JULIE RACH)

suspects your pet has scaly face, he or she will diagnose the condition by examining skin scrapings under a microscope.

Although scaly face has the potential to be a serious condition, the good news is that it can be easily treated by a veterinarian using Ivermectin, which will remove the mites and restore the skin to its normal appearance. Although some over-the-counter remedies are sold to treat scaly face, a veterinarian-supervised course of treatment using Ivermectin will alleviate the problem more quickly and more easily.

Stress

The appearance of white lines or small holes on the large feathers of a bird's wings and tail are an indication that the bird was experiencing stress as its feathers were developing. Not surprisingly, these lines or holes are referred to as "stress bars" or "stress lines." If you notice stress bars on your parrot's feathers, discuss them with your avian veterinarian. Be prepared to tell the doctor of anything new in your bird's routine because parrots are creatures of habit that sometimes react badly to changes in their surroundings, diet or daily activities.

I find stress bars on my bird's feathers each time she completes a course of antibiotic treatments, and I also find stress bars on her tail feathers regularly. I attribute the stress bars on her tail to the fact that she is a rather clumsy parrot and often catches or bends her developing tail feathers in the cage bars and floor grate.

This Amazon is recovering from an upper respiratory infection that caused it to rub its head excessively against the cage bars. Notice the dried debris around its cere and the clumpy feathers on the top of its head. (PHOTO BY GARY GALLERSTEIN, DVM)

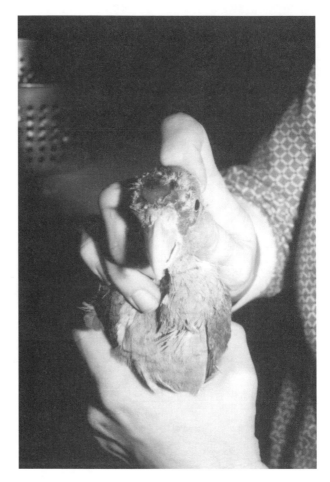

Vitamin A Deficiency

Vitamin A deficiency, or hypovitaminosis A, is another common health problem seen in pet birds that eat seed-only diets. Signs of vitamin A deficiency include respiratory problems, vision problems, mouth sores and frequent yeast infections. Treatment includes supplemental vitamin A injections and antibiotics to treat any additional infections the bird has.

Vitamin A deficiency can be easily prevented by feeding a bird a varied diet that includes dark orange and dark green vegetables, such as sweet potatoes, broccoli, carrots and red peppers, and fruits such as papaya, apricots and cantaloupe.

Upper Respiratory Infections

Upper respiratory infections are commonly seen in pet birds that eat seed-only diets without vitamin or fresh food supplements. Signs of an upper respiratory infection include nasal discharge, tail bobbing, watery eyes and fluffed feathers.

CARE WITH KISSES

To avoid the possible exposure to human saliva, please don't kiss your bird on the beak (kiss it on top of its little head instead). Do not allow your parrot to put its head into your mouth, nibble on your lips or preen your teeth. Although you may see birds doing this on television or in pictures in a magazine and think that it's a cute trick, it's unsafe for your bird's health and well-being. It could also leave you open to a nip on the lip, cheek or nose from your pet because your bird may not be in the mood to play this game with you.

Antibiotics prescribed by an avian veterinarian are in order to treat this condition in your pet bird. (Please don't use over-the-counter antibiotics to treat your bird for any illness because antibiotics only work on bacterial infections. To be effective, an antibiotic dosage must take into account the weight of the animal being treated, which is why you should use only medications prescribed by your bird's veterinarian.)

Poor Behavior or Poor Health?

If your bird suddenly begins misbehaving, make an appointment with your avian veterinarian for an evaluation. Some behavior problems indicate illness, and you want to rule out this possibility before beginning to resolve your bird's behavior problems.

You should also evaluate changes in your bird's environment—did you move its cage, change its feeding schedule or stop taking it out for playtimes? Remember that birds often do not react well to sudden changes in their routines, and they may react by misbehaving. If the behavioral problem persists after your avian veterinarian gives your pet a clean bill of health, you may need to consult an avian behaviorist for further assistance.

Avian behaviorists, also called parrot behavior consultants, help parrots and their owners better understand one another. They do this through lectures at conventions, through articles in magazines and on the Internet and through personal consultations on the telephone or in person. In a perfect world, the behaviorist would meet with new parrot owners while their parrot is still a chick in order to prevent the development of problem behaviors. However, many pet owners seek the advice of behaviorists only after problems have begun.

Avian behaviorists have learned how to address parrot behavior problems by studying bird behavior, dog and cat training techniques and human psychology. Some of them have worked in veterinary hospitals or raised birds, as well.

Parrot owners can find avian behaviorists online, through referrals from an avian veterinarian or through classified advertisements in bird specialty magazines and pet care newsletters and newspapers.

chapter 5

BEHAVIORS THAT INDICATE STRESS

Birds experience "positive" stress that produces excitement and enjoyment, such as a play session with a favored person or a ride in the car. However, stress frequently has negative ramifications and can cause illness and behavioral problems in your bird. A bird can be stressed by a number of things, even detecting tension in the home between partners. Stress can result from feeling insecure because its cage is in the center of the room. Birds need to feel secure in their

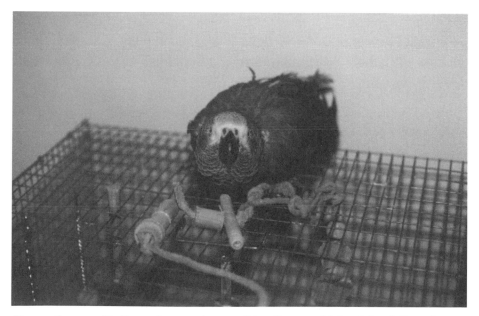

Be sure that your bird's cage is up against a solid wall to provide it with a feeling of security. (PHOTO BY JULIE RACH)

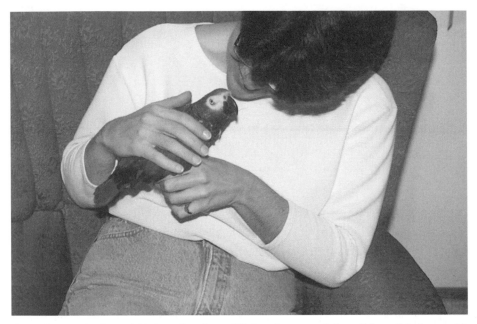

Sometimes, a frightened bird needs to be cuddled and reassured that all is well in its world.
(Photo by Julie Rach)

cages, so make sure that your bird's home has at least one solid wall behind it. A solid wall "protects" your bird from being approached from behind by predators and other scary things—it will help your bird to relax.

Ideally, your bird will encounter some combination of positive stress and negative stress throughout its life. Try to minimize the negative stress and provide some positive stress. It's impossible to remove all stresses from your bird's life, just as it's impossible to remove them from your own. However, by striking a balance, you can help your bird live a more comfortable, less stressed life.

Among the common stressors for birds are:

- new people in the home
- new pets in the home
- loud noises
- sudden movements
- earthquakes
- rearrangement of the furniture in the bird's room
- sensing stress in its owner's life
- dirty feathers
- attaining sexual maturity and being unable to breed
- boredom
- insecurity
- malnutrition
- lack of sleep
- loneliness
- lack of toys
- owner's reinforcement of feather picking

Some birds show fear by hiding in a corner of their cages. (PHOTO BY JULIE RACH)

Fear

Generally, frightened birds hold their feathers flat against their bodies and try to make themselves as "thin" as they can. They also stretch their necks, stare with small pupils and they may raise themselves off their perches. When the fear passes, the bird raises all its feathers and shakes them.

Birds can also show fear by puffing their feathers, screaming, growling, hiding, flying away from whatever has scared it, raising the crest (if the bird has one) or becoming aggressive.

To help calm your bird when it becomes scared, you can talk to it, cuddle it or cover your bird's cage. You will have to experiment to see which reaction your bird shows to things that frighten it and which kind of attention works best to allay your pet's fears.

Feather Picking

Stress can cause one of the most obvious behavior problems in parrots—feather picking. Some species, such as African greys, seem more prone to feather picking than others, but almost any parrot can develop this problem.

Don't confuse picking with normal preening. Once feather picking begins, it seems to be a compulsive habit. It actually calms some birds, even though it appears to us to be painful. Birds that suddenly begin picking their feathers, especially those under the wings, may have an intestinal parasite called *Giardia*. If you notice that your bird suddenly starts pulling its feathers out, contact your avian veterinarian for an evaluation.

For the first six years my African grey lived with me, she picked her feathers regularly. She came to me without anything more than downy underfeathers from just below her lower beak to her vent, and her crop was picked down to pink skin. By gradually changing a variety of factors in her life, she eventually learned to leave her feathers alone, though she still has a small bare area on her chest that may never be fully feathered, as it is likely that she damaged the feather follicles themselves with her picking.

The first step was to determine if there was a physical cause for her picking. When I knew that her health was relatively stable, my next step was to consistently provide a routine to my bird's life. I have put her cage in approximately the same place in each of the apartments we have lived in, set the same pieces of furniture around it and hung the same pieces of artwork on the walls over the cage. I have also made sure that she is served her meals at approximately the same time every day and that she receives consistent attention from me.

In addition to her routine, I offered my bird a varied and well-balanced diet that included some visually and (I hoped) mentally interesting items, such as corn on the cob, carrot sticks, zucchini wedges, pomegranate slices, green beans and pea pods. In this way, I believed I was not only feeding my bird's body, but also feeding her mind by giving her something interesting to play with in her food bowl.

Feather picking can occasionally progress to self-mutilation of a bird's skin.
(Photo by Gary A. Gallerstein, DVM)

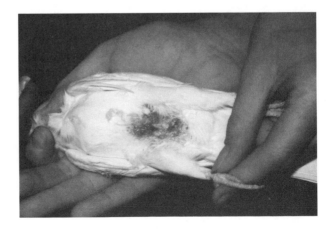

One of the biggest challenges was to encourage my bird to play. Perhaps she didn't have toys that interested her in her previous home, or maybe her health wasn't good enough to allow her to play, but she didn't seem to understand what toys were all about when she came to me. By spending time around a variety of birds at my friends' homes and at her veterinarian's office and through trial-and-error introduction by me, I eventually found some toys that interest her enough so that she destroys them and doesn't chew on her feathers quite so frequently.

In addition to stress, psychological causes for feather picking can include boredom, insecurity, breeding frustrations and nervousness. After Sindbad's veterinarian determined that her picking had a psychological cause, I began to look at the world through her eyes. What seemed strange or frightening? What was comforting and familiar? What had owners of other birds that picked found successful in helping their pets stop this habit? I soon discovered I had many more questions than answers, but I pressed on.

As much as I'd like to tell you differently, my efforts were neither overwhelmingly nor universally successful. Sindbad would leave her feathers alone for a week or so, then preen them down to the skin with a vengeance. Some weeks she would pull the feathers on her chest, while other weeks she would destroy the feathers on her back or the tips of her wings. It seemed that for every two steps of progress, she took three steps backward into more serious picking. Still I persevered. I knew that if she was still picking, something was not right in her universe, and I continued to try to find out what was making her so unsettled and insecure.

I didn't try using any of the spray-on products touted to be cures for feather picking. Birds preen their feathers to keep them clean, so if you apply something to that feather, the bird is going to work extra hard to clean the feather, even to the point of chewing the feather off! If you're going to spray anything on your bird, make sure it's no stronger than clean, warm water, and also be sure your bird enjoys being misted before you make this a regular part of its routine.

As her health improved, Sindbad's picking lessened. One day, I happened to notice that I had a mostly feathered bird—after only six years of work. I don't have a magic solution to offer except to ask that you have your bird evaluated by your avian veterinarian if it starts to pick, and if the cause isn't physical, please be patient with your feather-picking parrot as you try to distract it away from its feathers.

Freezing

In the wild, birds often "freeze" in position to avoid being seen by predators. If a bird is new to your home, it may react like this the first few times you come in the room, or a longtime pet may react this way to new people. With time and patient conditioning on the owner's part, most birds get over this behavior.

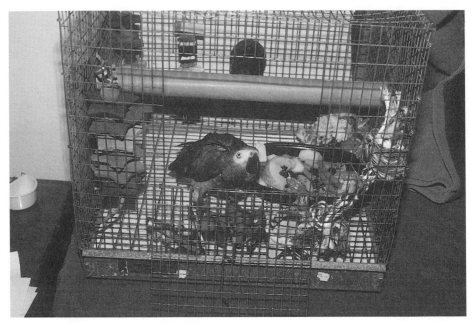

Stress can come from a variety of situations. Some well-meaning pet owners may actually cause their birds to experience stress by overcrowding their birds' cages with toys, food and other distractions. (PHOTO BY JULIE RACH)

Growling

If your cockatiel or African grey growls, it's because the bird is afraid of something in its environment. The bird growls in an attempt to scare away the frightening intruder.

Hissing

Like growling, hissing is an attempt to frighten off something perceived to be threatening by your bird. Cockatiels are more likely to hiss than other birds, and some will rock back and forth in addition to the hissing. Both are defensive gestures.

Nail Biting

Just as some people bite their nails when they're nervous or worried about something, so do some parrots.

Panting

Panting can indicate physical problems, such as heat stroke. However, it can also be an indication of stress. Once you're sure the bird doesn't have heat stroke, evaluate its environment to see what's upsetting your bird, then take steps to remedy the situation.

Screaming

As mentioned earlier, parrots are great reflectors of their owners' moods. Screaming is one of the most common ways that they express their sense of their owner's stress.

If your parrot suddenly starts screaming, take a moment to assess your own situation. Did you have a bad day at work? Did you just have an argument with your spouse? Did one of your teenagers just test the limits of your patience again? If the answer to any of these questions is "Yes," here's another one: Are you taking the stress you feel at these other situations out on your parrot? Walk away from your parrot, calm down and take a few deep breaths. After you're calm, go back and see your parrot. Talk to it in a bright and cheery tone. Chances are your bird will sense the change in your mood and will react accordingly.

In other cases, a screaming bird is stressed about something in its environment. It could be that the bird is reacting to a wild bird sitting on the rail of your back porch, or it could be that another bird in the home is misbehaving. In extreme cases, the toaster could be overheating or a pan on the stove may have caught fire. If your otherwise quiet bird suddenly starts screaming, you should investigate to determine the cause before you discipline your parrot.

Finally, birds sometimes need to be reassured that they aren't alone and that you really do still care about them. If your parrot screams to you from one end of the house, simply call back, "I'm here. Are you okay?" Your bird will feel better knowing where you are and will probably go back to its normal routine. Be sure to tell your bird, "I'll be right back," or, "I'm just going in the other room," when you leave its room. This will help your bird understand that you aren't abandoning it.

To prevent screaming from becoming a problem, don't reward your bird for screaming. If you reward it by yelling back or providing it with some other dramatic reinforcement, you will simply be training your intelligent pet to scream again the next time it wants attention. If your bird screams, simply tell it to be quiet in a calm tone. If that doesn't work, a quick dirty look may do the trick. If those solutions don't resolve the problem, simply ignore the bird when it screams and praise it lavishly when it behaves in an acceptable manner. Because parrots like attention from their human companions, they will quickly catch on to this game.

Finally, accept the fact that your bird is going to be a little loud from time to time. It may want to greet the dawn and bid the sunset adieu, or it may just feel very good at some point in the day and want to scream a little! Knowing this from the start will help you accept the occasional outbursts from your pet.

Restraint collars should be applied to feather-picking birds under the guidance of a veterinarian. Before applying a collar, the veterinarian should try to determine the underlying cause for the picking.
(PHOTO BY GARY A. GALLERSTEIN, DVM)

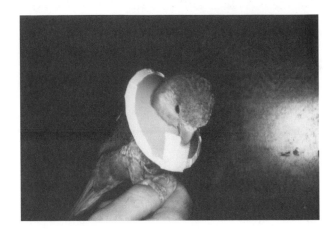

Self-Mutilation

As noted above, birds under stress may pick their feathers. In more extreme cases, the birds begin chewing on or picking at their legs, toes and chests. Veterinary care is often required to help alleviate this condition. Treatment may include the application of an Elizabethan collar to keep the bird from picking itself, surgery to repair skin damage or behavior-modifying medication.

Shaking

Shaking can indicate seizures or other medical problems, or it could simply be a sign of a parrot that's afraid of something in its environment. If your bird is not prone to seizures, you will need to assess its environment to see what could be causing the stress that makes it shake.

chapter 6

BEHAVIORS THAT INDICATE BOREDOM

Because birds are such intelligent creatures, they can become bored fairly easily, and they can indicate this in a number of ways, including feather picking, shredding paper, overeating, screaming or destroying your possessions.

In some cases, parrot owners don't do much to help the situation, keeping their birds in what is essentially solitary confinement. Pet parrots like to be part of the action, so don't put your bird's cage in an isolated part of the house or a room that you only use occasionally. Breeding birds may need privacy and some peace and quiet, so they can be housed in rooms that aren't used frequently, but

Birds that live in solitary confinement may develop behavioral problems because of boredom.
(Photo by Julie Rach)

single pet parrots should be kept in the family room, living room or den where they can be a part of family activities.

Chewing

Chewing and destroying things around the home are often the activities of a bored bird. I know a cockatoo who showed how bored he was by destroying his owners' television remote control and two cordless phones in the space of a few weeks. By giving him some discipline and some boundaries for behavior, his owners channeled his energy away from these destructive behaviors. They challenged his mental abilities with new and better toys, they supervised his every move when he was out of the cage and disciplined him when he looked as if he was going to chew on something that was off limits. They gave him a wider variety of foods to entertain him and even made eating a challenge by offering him nuts in the shell that he had to open and pea pods that he had to split in order to retrieve the peas.

Feather picking has many causes, including a monotonous diet, boredom, stress, sexual frustration and physical illness. Notice the bald spot in the middle of Sindbad's chest. (PHOTO BY JULIE RACH)

Amazon owners need to monitor the amount of fat that their birds consume— Amazons are natural snackers and can rapidly become overweight. Oil seeds, such as sunflower or safflower seeds, and nuts are common sources of dietary fat for pet birds. (PHOTO BY GARY A. GALLERSTEIN, DVM)

Feather Picking

Boredom is one of several reasons that may cause a bird to pick its feathers. If your bird suddenly begins picking its feathers and no medical cause for the picking is found, there is a good chance that your bird is reacting to a lack of interesting things in its life. Feather picking is comforting to the parrot (although the behavior looks painful to us). Some birds pick small areas of feathers, such as their legs, while others start on their chests and pick down to their vents. Regular opportunities to exercise can reduce or eliminate feather picking in some parrots.

As discussed previously, the cause of feather picking must be found before the problem can be resolved. You may need to work with your avian veterinarian and/or avian behaviorist to make this determination.

Although Sindbad looks as if she's in trouble here, she's not. Hanging upside down is a game she plays to indicate that she is content with the world. (PHOTO BY JULIE RACH)

Overeating

Overeating is a common behavior in budgies that have been neglected by their owners. These birds never come out of their cages to exercise or interact with their owners, but their owners often ease their guilty consciences by offering the birds lots of treats, including millet.

Oil seeds are a food that budgies love, but they are high in fat and can make a pet bird obese if it is allowed to indulge in them to its heart's content. If you notice that your bird's breastbone has suddenly disappeared into rolls of fat, it's becoming overweight and needs to exercise and interact with you. Amazons and some species of cockatoos can also become overweight easily, so watch these birds for signs of obesity.

You can consider a bird obese if you can see bald patches in its feathers. These are created by fat deposits under the skin that cause the feathers to part. Overweight birds also may stand with their feet wide apart, or you may be able to see rolls of fat across the bird's abdomen, along its flanks and inner thighs, and around its crop. A little fat in these locations is acceptable, but large amounts of fat are not. Ask your veterinarian for more information on how you can determine if your pet bird is overweight.

Obesity can cause a bird to develop heart disease, fatty tumors, respiratory distress during exercise or egg-binding. An overweight bird is also at higher risk to suffer complications if it has to be anesthetized.

Paper Shredding

Another common behavior associated with parrot boredom is paper shredding. Parrots that have access to the paper that lines their cage trays often shred it because they have energy to burn and nothing else to do.

You can make this paper shredding into a game: Provide your parrot with a variety of chewable paper items, including subscription cards from magazines, index cards or the empty tube from a roll of paper towels or toilet paper. Hold these up for your bird's inspection and destruction. It's a simple way to spend time with your parrot and help it burn off some excess energy. Your pet can perform this shredding routine while it sits on the arm of your chair as you read a magazine or watch TV. Your bird will appreciate the attention, and you'll enjoy watching it chew up the things you offer!

If you have a peach-faced lovebird that suddenly starts shredding paper and tucking the strips into its rump feathers, it's not bored. This is an instinctive behavior in females that indicates an interest in nest building. In the wild, female peachies gather twigs and small strips of bark from trees, tuck them into their rump feathers with both ends showing and fly off to a nest site. In your home, your lovebird may gather strips of newspaper, toothpicks or other small items in an attempt to build a nest in her cage.

Refusing to Eat

Although some bored birds overeat, others become extremely fussy eaters. To help prevent this, you may need to be creative in how and what you feed your bird. You may want to offer your parrot some tempting treats on a skewer or rod feeder, stuff goodies into the openings of a pine cone (some companies offer commercially made versions) or vary the food choices in its dish to encourage it to take an interest in eating again.

Restlessness

A bird that is temporarily bored with a situation (for example, it's had enough cuddling and wants to go play on its cage) will become fidgety and restless. Your relationship with your pet will thrive if you pay attention to signs of restlessness and accommodate your bird. If you don't, it may even bite you out of frustration!

Preventing Boredom

To help keep your bird from being bored and beginning some of these behaviors, you can play games with your parrot. Energy expended in playing, either by itself or with you, is energy that your formerly bored parrot won't channel into otherwise destructive acts. The following games are particularly effective pastimes for medium and large parrots, such as Amazons, African greys, cockatoos and macaws.

Shell Game   Play a variation on the old "shell game" from the carnival sideshow. In the avian version, you can hide a favorite treat under a nut cup or paper muffin cup and let your bird guess which shell hides the prize.

Great Escape   Offer your bird a clean, knotted-up piece of rope or vegetable-tanned leather and see how long it takes your pet to untie the knots. Give your bird extra points if it doesn't chew through any of the knots to untie them.

Mechanic   Give your parrot a clean nut and bolt with the nut screwed on and see how long it takes your bird to undo the nut. Make sure the nut and bolt are large enough that your pet won't swallow either accidentally while playing.

Peek-a-boo   This is one of my bird's favorites. I put a beach towel loosely over her and her cage top, then let her work her way out from under the towel and to the edge of the cage top. She's come to expect the cuddling and lavish praise I use to reward her for being so clever as to find her way out every time.

Some parrots like to play peek-a-boo with their owners. (PHOTO BY JULIE RACH)

Tug-of-war   Give your bird one end of an empty paper towel roll and tug gently. Chances are your parrot won't easily let go, or if it does, it will quickly be back for more! If your bird is naturally aggressive, you shouldn't let it "win" too frequently, but if it's naturally shy, let it "win" often to build its confidence.

In addition to these games, you can also take your bird out of its cage and dance with it. Your bird can dance by itself on its cage top or play gym, or you and your bird can dance together. My parrot especially likes peppy, up-tempo oldies such as "Gimme Some Lovin'," "Your Momma Don't Dance" and "Rescue Me."

You can also hold the bird out at arm's length and let it flap its wings. You may have to lift and lower the bird slowly a few times to give it a hint of what you want it to do. Let your bird flap until it appears to be just a little winded, and build up its stamina by extending the exercise periods slightly each day. This exercise is particularly good for Amazons and rose-breasted cockatoos, which can be prone to obesity. Be sure you are standing away from ceiling fans, low-hanging lamps and other objects that could harm your bird while it's flapping.

Your bird may have some games of its own to play with you. Many parrots enjoy "accidentally" knocking things off their cage tops to watch their owners bend over to fetch the dropped item. Don't be surprised if your parrot makes you play this game with some frequency. Some birds entertain themselves by getting into apparently hazardous situations, such as hanging from their cage ceilings by a single toe, just to be rescued by their owners.

chapter 7

BREEDING
BEHAVIORS

All parrot owners eventually learn that birds are governed by their hormones. Some birds get through breeding season without harming themselves or their owners too badly, while other parrots become biting, screaming, feather-picking monsters until their hormones subside.

When parrots reach sexual maturity and breeding season rolls around, most of them are motivated to mate. However, most pet birds have no bird to mate with, so they try to mate with their owners, perches, toys or other objects. If you see your bird mount an object and rub its vent against it, it's demonstrating mating behavior. Some birds cluck or honk while mating.

The good news is that if your bird feels like mating, you're providing for it well. Mating is something that birds do only when all conditions are right. There must be a sufficient, steady supply of food and water, the bird must be in good health and it must feel comfortable and secure in its environment. Only healthy birds mate—sick birds don't have the strength or the energy for it.

Signs of Maturity

Aggression

Aggression can take many forms. Breeding birds may bite their owners, may defend their cages fiercely or they may become overly protective of their food dishes. In many species, male birds are more aggressive than females, but in eclectus and some types of parrotlets, the female is the more aggressive member of the pair.

This cockatoo may be defending its territory. Notice how its crest is raised and its body feathers are fluffed to make it appear larger. (PHOTO BY PAMELA L. HIGDON)

Biting

Mature birds may bite their owners to protect their cages and territories. They may also bite their owners' significant others for daring to pay attention to the owner that the bird has selected as its substitute mate, or they may bite their owners for having the nerve to pay attention to a human mate. Mature birds also bite to defend their food bowls. They often give indications—eye pinning, tail fanning, growling—that their owners shouldn't push their luck. However, some owners don't take the hint and get bitten.

Display Behavior

If it's late winter or spring and your bird suddenly starts strutting, screaming, singing, flapping its wings and generally trying to draw attention to itself, chances are it's a male bird that's displaying in order to attract a mate and scare off other males. If your bird has a crest, it will raise it frequently during display periods.

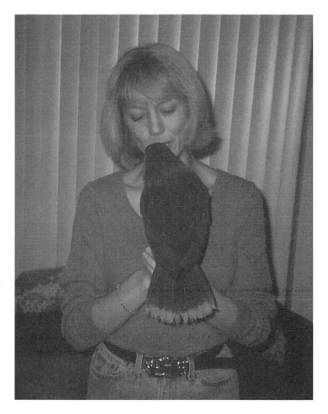

Although most display behavior is credited to male birds, some female birds display for their favored people during breeding season. (Photo by Pamela L. Higdon)

Egg Binding

Egg binding is a breeding problem that requires urgent veterinary attention. A hen is egg-bound if she is unable to lay an egg that is stuck in the oviduct. The causes of egg binding can include an oversized or soft-shelled egg, stress, low blood calcium levels or overbreeding. If left untreated, egg binding can cause kidney, intestinal or urinary problems. It can also develop into a life-threatening situation.

If you see a hen panting, paralyzed on the cage floor, straining to lay an egg or if you see an egg partially out of the cloaca, the hen is egg-bound. She will need to be placed in a small, warm cage (about 85° F) in a humid room, such as a bathroom with a hot shower running. Sometimes heat and humidity are enough to help an egg-bound hen pass the egg, but in other cases, further veterinary care is required. Once you have placed your hen in a warm and humid environment, contact your veterinarian for further instructions.

Egg Laying

A single pet bird will lay eggs without a male bird being present. These eggs are clear and will not hatch. If your bird lays eggs, it means that she is healthy

Your bird may demonstrate its interest in breeding by surprising you with an egg. (Photo by Julie Rach)

and content. Egg laying can be quite a shock to some owners. I know because my parrot presented me with eggs after being a pet in my home for more than eight years. She did not lay eggs in her previous home, so it was a bit unsettling to uncover her cage one morning and see what appeared to be an off-white Ping-Pong ball in her cage.

To discourage egg laying, some experts would advise to remove the eggs from the cage as they are laid. Others would recommend leaving the clutch intact until the hen completes her laying. In extreme cases of egg laying, hormone treatments may be needed to stop the bird's body from creating the eggs. Consult your avian veterinarian for his or her suggestions on how to stop your parrot from laying eggs.

Feather Picking

Birds that are sexually mature may take out their frustrations at being denied the opportunity to breed by pulling their feathers. In extreme cases, the birds may also indulge in self-mutilation of their chests or feet.

Separated lovebirds may pick their feathers in frustration and loneliness, pining for their mates. When reunited, the birds appear to be pleased to see their formerly missing companion. Lovebirds were, in fact, named for their common practice of clumping or cuddling together as if they were in love with the bird closest to them on the perch or tree branch. Lovebirds groom their neighbors constantly and cuddle or snuggle with them.

Masturbation

If you notice your bird rubbing its vent against a favorite toy or against your hand, it's working off its sexual frustration. You can curb your bird's behavior by removing the toy that is the object of its affections. You can also allow your bird to burn off excess energy by exercising outside its cage, such as climbing, flapping or chasing a toy that you're dragging across the floor.

You may also need to change the way you handle your bird during breeding season. Don't rub a bird's lower back or under its wings during this time because you may trigger a breeding response. In many cases, these signals do not cause any harm to bird or owner, but if your bird becomes aggressive during breeding season, be careful about how you handle it during this time.

Mutual Preening

Mutual preening is a behavior that bonded pairs demonstrate. In mutual preening, members of the pair will sit close to each other and one bird will preen the other's neck and the top of its head—areas the bird being preened cannot reach itself.

Nest Building

Although parrots do not build nests in the traditional sense, they may start looking for small, dark nooks and crannies in your home in which to lay eggs. Some birds like to inspect kitchen cupboards and may start trying to nest in your pots and pans, while other birds will attempt to make nests in cubbyholes of rolltop desks. Still others may check out your linen closets, looking for a warm, soft place among your sheets and towels. If you notice your bird has developed a sudden preoccupation with dark, out-of-the-way places, it may be indicating its willingness to breed.

Pair Bonding

Pair bonding helps parrots successfully raise chicks. Indications of pair bonding include mutual preening, mutual feeding, defense of the mate and of the birds' home territory.

Because parrot chicks generally take several months to raise, there needs to be a bond between the parent birds to ensure that both parent birds take an

Bonded pairs of birds often conduct themselves in unison. (Photo by Julie Rach)

interest in raising the chicks. In some species, the male birds share incubating duties, while in others, the male feeds the female bird while she sits on the eggs, guards the entrance to the nest and feeds the chicks after they hatch.

The pair bond is also part of a pet bird's charm because the pair bond fosters loyalty and affection between parrots and their owners. At the onset of sexual maturity, this pair bond between parrot and owner may be trying because the bird may consider its owner as its mate. When it does, it will preen the owner, attempt to feed him or her and vigorously defend the owner against all interlopers (including spouses and other family members) by biting either the owner or the interloper.

Not all parrots perceive their owners as mates, and not all parrots defend their owners during breeding season. These behaviors are discussed because they *can* occur, not because they *will*.

Paper Shredding

Peach-faced lovebirds are particularly prone to this behavior. Females shred long strips of paper, tuck them in their rump feathers and fly off in search of a potential nesting site.

Regurgitating Food

Regurgitation in a healthy bird is a courting behavior in parrots. Males regurgitate to females and to chicks, and young parrots regurgitate to each other.

If your bird regurgitates to you, you can calmly return it to its cage or play gym to allow it to settle down. You can also distract it with a favorite toy. I generally thank my parrot for her kind thoughts but let her know that I'm fixing my own meal soon. This way, I believe she knows that I appreciate her gesture and am not appalled by it.

Regurgitation can also indicate a variety of physical problems, including crop infections, a blockage in the digestive tract, thyroid gland enlargement or proventricular dilatation syndrome. If your bird appears ill and regurgitates, contact your avian veterinarian.

Screaming

Parrots under the influence of their hormones are prone to screaming fits during breeding season. If your bird becomes extremely vocal, you can try to distract it with a favored toy, you can cover its cage for about ten minutes to give it a "time-out" or you can expose the bird to new experiences, such as play time in a different room or a ride in the car.

Displaced Affection

On occasion, pet birds treat their human "mates" no differently than they would parrot mates. One spring, a friend of mine who owns a male Eleanora cockatoo showed up at her doctor's office sporting a collection of bruises, slashes and other marks of potential abuse. The doctor immediately suspected abuse, and she was being abused, but not by any human member of the household. Her cockatoo had chosen her as his mate and he was taking out his frustrations at not being able to breed with her.

In the spring, after the bird reached sexual maturity at about age 5, my friend was subjected to increasing amounts of abuse from her pet. What started as an amusing display of crest raising and tail spreading soon turned into fits of flying at her face in a threatening manner. This behavior lasted about three months.

The following year, the behavior got worse and lasted longer, culminating in the onslaught of bites and scratches that my friend's doctor saw when she sought treatment for an unrelated sinus infection.

Height is power in the bird world. Birds that are allowed to be taller than their owners may be difficult to manage. (PHOTO BY PAMELA L. HIGDON)

After this particular spring, my friend sought the assistance of avian behaviorist Sally Blanchard, who made some suggestions for behavior modification. Now the bird is not allowed to sit on my friend's shoulder. This was once his favorite perch, but he is too difficult to control when he's up there. He also is not allowed to perch on any item higher than my friend's chest level. He used to enjoy sitting on the bar at the top of the shower stall, for example, but the height gives him too much power and makes him even more difficult to control.

The bird has also been reintroduced to the concept of the "up" command, and he comes out of his cage only when he's on his best behavior. Previously, he was allowed out every day when his owners came home from work, whether he was behaving or not. His owners now look him in the eye and calmly tell him, "No" when he misbehaves, and they put him back in his cage for "time-out" if he becomes difficult to handle and manage.

Not only did my friend's health and appearance improve after she took control of her cockatoo's behavior, but his behavior and appearance seemed to improve, too. He had a history of picking the tops of his wings every spring, but he stopped pulling those feathers after my friend instituted stronger control over his life.

Breeding Basics

Many parrot species are difficult to sex visually. Males essentially look like females, which can make setting up true breeding pairs impossible. Although some longtime breeders can obtain a fair degree of accuracy by observing their birds, pet owners and novice breeders shouldn't try to visually sex their birds, or you may end up like me, who had my so-called "male" bird lay eggs after being a pet for 16 years.

Many parrot species cannot be sexed visually, which can make setting up breeding pairs quite challenging. (PHOTO BY GARY A. GALLERSTEIN, DVM)

If you are going to set up birds for breeding, the following sexing methods are available: observation, DNA sexing, surgical sexing, fecal analysis and feather sexing. Brief descriptions of these methods follow:

1. Observation is generally an unreliable method. I discovered my "male" parrot's gender when "he" laid an egg!

2. DNA sexing analyzes red blood cells to determine whether male or female chromosomes are present in your bird. Your veterinarian takes a blood sample from your bird and sends it to a laboratory for examination. Results are available in about three weeks.

3. Surgical sexing requires that a small incision is made in the bird's side under anesthesia. A veterinarian inserts an endoscope into the incision to look for either an ovary if the bird is female or a testicle if the bird is male. Although it might seem risky, surgical sexing is quite safe if performed by an experienced avian veterinarian.

4. Fecal analysis examines a small sample of the bird's droppings for the presence of reproductive hormones. This test is only effective with sexually mature birds.

5. Feather sexing looks at feather pulp from a blood feather for the presence of sex chromosomes. The feather is kept on ice and sent to a laboratory by overnight mail for evaluation.

Your avian veterinarian can further discuss these sexing methods with you and help you decide which is the best one to use on your breeder birds.

Breeding Small Parrots

Cockatiels are very popular pet birds and provide a good illustration of what to expect if you would like to breed your birds. They are also one species that you can sex visually. Cockatiels develop their adult plumage at about 6 months of age, and the differences in gender become apparent at that time. Many breeders can distinguish the males from the females before this point, however, as males begin to vocalize when they are about 3 months of age, while females remain relatively quiet.

In traditional gray birds, males will have lemon yellow feathers on their faces, foreheads, cheeks and throats, and their orange cheek patches will be brighter than those of the female birds. The facial feathers of traditional gray female birds will have a gray wash to them, and the cheek patches will be smaller and duller. Females will also show barred feathers on their backs, rumps and tails.

In color mutations, male cinnamons and fallows develop their characteristic yellow masks and lose their barred tail feathers, while the females have duller facial feathers and retain their barred feathers. Whitefaced males have (as their name suggests) white faces, while female whitefaces actually have grayish faces and the characteristic barring on their tail feathers.

In lutinos, you can distinguish males by the lack of barred feathers on their wing and tail feathers, but you must examine the birds closely to determine if its feathers are barred or not, as the yellow bars are often hard to see against the lutino's white feather background.

Pearls and pieds are difficult to sex visually because their mutations hide some of the characteristic colors and patterns. Pearl males may or may not lose their spots as they mature, and many ultimately look like standard gray males after their first molts. Pearl females retain gray facial feathers, while pearl males have light faces.

Even more challenging to sex visually are the albinos. Both sexes are pure white and lack the characteristic yellow masks or orange cheek patches used to differentiate males and females of other mutations. In these cases, other methods of determining gender, such as feather sexing, DNA analysis or surgical sexing may be required.

Once you've established which of your birds are male and which are female, consider their strengths and weaknesses. You want to be sure to create breeding pairs for good reasons, so you may want to put two birds with outstanding pet qualities together, or you may want to try to improve the color or pattern of future generations by pairing two prime examples of a particular mutation.

After you've selected your pairs, you'll need to think about nest boxes for your growing flock. Any nest box larger than 10 inches by 10 inches in the box floor should work well for raising cockatiels. Many breeders set their birds up with boxes that measure 12 inches high by 12 inches wide by 12 inches deep. The box should feature a perch slightly below the box opening on both the interior and exterior of the box. Having a perch on the inside helps parent birds get in and out of the box easier, and it also offers them a site from which to feed growing chicks.

The box should also have a viewing hole so you can check on the progress of the chicks without disturbing the parent birds too much. If you house your breeding birds in an aviary, be sure to provide two or three more nest boxes than you have pairs. Females will fight over the boxes, which can lead to decreased egg production because the birds are more interested in squabbling over territory than they are in laying eggs.

You can have a definite impact on your birds' breeding success. Aviary disturbances by people or other animals, along with excessive handling of breeding birds, can cause birds not to mate. These activities can also chase nesting birds off eggs or cause parent birds to abandon their chicks in the nest.

Ensure that all perches in the breeding cage are secure. Your birds will likely mate on their perches, and loose perches can result in infertile eggs because your birds are unable to mate successfully on unsteady footing.

You'll know your selections were successful when you hear your male birds whistling and see them flying around or chasing the females. The males may bow, nod or chirp at their mates, while the females will indicate their readiness to breed by crouching low on perches with their tails up and their crests down. The male will then proceed to mate with the female, and eggs will follow in about seven to ten days. During the interval between mating and egg-laying, you will probably notice that the female spends an unusual amount of time in the nest box and devours cuttlebones and other calcium supplements eagerly.

Five eggs is the average cockatiel clutch size, although hens can lay anywhere from 2 to 15 eggs. Eggs are laid on an alternate day schedule, and will hatch in the order in which they were laid. If you see more than ten eggs in a box, you should suspect that two hens are laying simultaneously in the same box, although some breeders have reported as many as 15 fertile eggs being produced by a pair in a single clutch.

The parent birds will start to incubate the eggs after the hen has laid at least two. The parents share incubating duties, with the male bird usually setting on the eggs during the day and the female taking the night shift.

While the parents are incubating their eggs, be sure to provide them with a water dish. Although cockatiels aren't usually enthusiastic bathers, many parent birds appreciate the chance to soak their feathers during this time because wet feathers can help raise the humidity in the nest box. Having a humid atmosphere in the box helps chicks hatch more easily by softening the eggshells slightly.

During incubation, parent birds will keep the nest box immaculately clean. Don't be alarmed to see some monstrous droppings from your parent birds because they will wait to defecate until they are well away from the nest box.

Chicks, however, will defecate in the box after they hatch, so breeders need to pay attention to nest box lining and to the chicks' toes, which can become damaged from being caked with feces.

The parents will sit on the eggs for about 19 days before the chicks start to hatch. Cockatiels turn their eggs about every 30 minutes during the day and about every 90 minutes or so during the night. If you should have to incubate eggs artificially, keep this time frame in mind or else the developing chick could become stuck to the albumen in the egg and die.

When the chicks hatch, they are covered with a yellowish down. Whitefaces and albinos, of course, have white down. Other mutations, such as the lutino and fallow, can be identified by their red eyes, which appear as pink bulges under closed lids.

Chicks take 36 to 48 hours to hatch. They start by rotating within the eggshell and breaking the shell around the middle from the inside. The chick's head is in the large, rounded end of the egg during hatching, and you can hear it chirp (or pip) as it makes its way into the world.

After the chicks hatch, try not to open the nest box for inspection when the parent birds are inside because they could scramble for cover and injure the chicks inadvertently. To move the parents out of the way, tap lightly on the side of the nest box or offer them a favored treat in the main cage.

The following chronology will help you appreciate how quickly cockatiel chicks mature:

1 to 3 days   Chicks are covered with yellow down. They have naked heads and pink feet, skin, beaks and ceres. Their eyes are closed, and they weigh about 4 grams (.15 ounce) and measure about 3 cm (1.25 inches) in length. They will huddle with their clutchmates for warmth and support with their heads tucked inward and their bottoms pointed up and out.

4 days   Eyes begin to open.

5 days   Chicks begin to vocalize when begging for food.

9 days   Contour feathers begin to appear. First evidence of crest feathers.

10 days   Baby cockatiels hiss when disturbed.

12 days   Chick loses the egg tooth on the end of its beak.

15 days   Upper and lower mandibles of the beak become hard.

19 days   Orange cheek patches are evident in birds that will have them. Chicks also raise crests and spread wings when disturbed.

21 days   Chicks can now be handled daily to develop their pet qualities. Now is the time to start teaching them how wonderful being rubbed lightly on the back of the neck feels! Chicks will also start grasping at things with their feet, so be careful that they don't injure themselves while exploring.

30 days Chicks will look very much like their parents, having attained adult weight of 90 grams.

35 days Chicks begin to fledge (grow the feathers they will need to fly). Hen may begin laying next clutch of eggs as the younger chicks prepare to fledge.

40 days Chicks are usually weaned and eating on their own. Scatter seed on the floor and place extra seed dishes in the cage as chicks make the transition to feeding themselves. Watch the chicks to be sure they are really eating, not just playing with food.

50 days Large feathers on the chicks have become keratinous.

90 days First molt. The chick's beak turns dark gray.

270 days The chick has become sexually mature and attained its adult plumage.

Adult birds can raise two clutches a year and should be allowed to rest to maintain their good health. Cockatiel hens can lay eggs for eight to ten years, but the fertility decreases as the bird ages. Male cockatiels are fertile for 12 to 14 years.

Breeding Problems

Excessive egg laying can be a problem in cockatiels, and some female birds will lay eggs without a male bird being present. Unfortunately, this problem is not always easy to solve. Some excessive egg layers benefit by being put in breeding programs, while other birds can be "cycled out" of egg laying by allowing them to lay one clutch and incubate it for the normal time period. Still other birds cycle out of egg laying by having the nest "destroyed" by the owner removing all the eggs to simulate predation or other natural disasters.

More persistent egg layers may require a series of hormone shots from a veterinarian to solve the problem. Be aware that repeated series of these injections may cause health problems, such as obesity, increased water intake, increased urination and diabetes. Finally, some birds may need a hysterectomy to resolve their egg-laying problems. This operation is rather complex and unlike altering pet dogs and cats, it is not recommended as a standard course of action for pet birds.

If you have a hen that lays excessive eggs, make sure to supplement her diet with calcium and have mineral blocks and cuttlebone available to her. Egg-laying hens that do not have access to supplemental calcium will use the calcium in their own bones to create eggshells for their eggs, which can lead to fractures and other complications for the hen.

Infertility is a problem that many breeders face at some point in their careers. Infertility can be caused by parent birds that are too young or too old to breed successfully; unsteady perches in the breeding cage; an underlying health

APPROXIMATE BREEDING AGES FOR SOME COMMONLY KEPT PET PARROTS

Budgies, cockatiels and lovebirds—1 year

Conures—1½ to 2 years

Lories—2 to 3 years

Pionus, small cockatoos and macaws—2 to 4 years

African greys, Amazons and large cockatoos—3 to 6 years

problem, such as a bacterial or fungal infection in the parent birds; pair incompatibility; pet birds that are unable or unwilling to bond with another bird; an inadequate number of nest boxes; a poor diet for the parent birds; or an overly aggressive hen.

Some birds fail to incubate their eggs. Frightening events, such as earthquakes or rodents in the aviary, can cause birds to abandon their eggs. An unbonded pair of parent birds may also fail to incubate.

Some parent birds pick their chicks' feathers. If one of your pairs begins to pick their babies, you may have to foster the chicks out to other pairs. In some cases, the male bird is the culprit, which means that he should be removed from the breeding cage when the chicks start to feather out. The female can usually finish raising the chicks on her own. If this occurs, you may choose to remove the picking parents from your breeding program.

Although it seems odd to us, it is common for parent birds to eat their eggs. If you choose to use an egg eater in your breeding program, you will need to take away each egg as it is laid and replace it with an artificial one. Sometimes the egg-eating desire resolves once the hen starts to brood her clutch. However, birds that are confirmed egg eaters should not be bred.

Breeding Larger Parrots

Conures breed fairly well in captivity and provide a good example of what you will need to do to breed larger parrots. Set up your conures in breeding pairs, one pair per cage. Although the Patagonian conure will breed in a colony setting (several pairs together in a large aviary or flight), other conure species do not do well in colony settings.

Most conure species breed in the spring and summer, and some seem to be stimulated to breed by regular rainfall. Proper light and temperature are also key to breeding success. If your birds are kept indoors, you may have to provide them with supplemental light. One way to do so is to hang a Vitalite over their cage. When the indoor temperature reaches about 75°F and the birds are exposed to about 15 hours of light daily, their breeding cycles should be triggered.

Conures like small nesting spaces. The ideal small conure nest box is a vertical enclosure that measures 10 inches by 10 inches by 18 inches. Larger species favor a nest box that measures 12 inches by 12 inches by 24 inches. The box entrance is at the top, and an inspection panel on the side will allow you to check on the eggs and chicks without overly disturbing the parent birds. Line the box with pine shavings, and place it in the upper rear of the cage or aviary to provide security for the breeding pair.

Although it may seem obvious, be sure to select only healthy birds for your breeding program. The process of breeding and raising chicks puts a tremendous strain on a bird's body, so it's important to start with strong, healthy birds. Also, quarantine any new arrivals to your breeding program for at least one month to ensure that no diseases are spread in your aviary. Feed these birds last and with separate food and water bowls from the rest of your flock to prevent transmitting any diseases from the new birds to existing breeders in your collection.

When selecting your breeding pairs, make sure that you have pure pairs of the same species of conure. Conures can and will hybridize (breed with birds outside their own species), but aviculturists discourage such pairings. By mixing species in your breeding program, the resulting chicks will have diluted bloodlines and will not further the preservation of the birds' unique genetic heritage for the future.

To set up your breeding pairs, put all potential mates together in a large aviary, if possible, and let the birds pair off on their own. If you have two birds in a large cage in your living room and they've demonstrated a pair bond (for example, sitting close to one another, preening each other or feeding one another), they've already established their relationship and are good candidates for going to nest.

Once you've introduced a pair to each other, try not to separate those birds because forming a strong pair bond between the parent birds is crucial to breeding success. Remember that newly paired-up birds may not have viable eggs in their first season together, so you must give your breeding pairs ample time together (more than one breeding season) to determine if the pair will produce young. Although it may be tempting to split up infertile pairs after a fruitless breeding season, you must be patient and give the birds an opportunity to get accustomed to each other before determining their success or failure as parents.

If you will be keeping more than one pair of breeding conures in your home, don't stack the breeding cages on top of each other. Some birds become quite disturbed by the action of cage cleaning above or below them, and this could cause your parent birds to injure themselves by flying into the wire, or they could damage the eggs while scrambling in or out of the nest box.

One of the first steps a breeding pair of conures will take is to begin gnawing at the nest box. The hen will do most of the gnawing, although the male may join her in her efforts. Some conures will chew on their nest boxes so extensively that they destroy the boxes completely. If your birds are enthusiastic chewers, make sure the nest box has a double floor, or consider giving these birds a metal nest box with a wooden lining.

You can tell when your pair is ready to lay eggs if you see the female staying in the nest box most of the time, if both members of the pair are more aggressive at feeding time, if the male feeds the female more frequently or if the female's lower abdomen appears swollen. Sometimes you will see the birds mating on a perch in the cage, while at other times they will mate in the nest box. Check the nest box daily using the inspection door to see how many eggs your birds have laid.

To determine if you have viable eggs, you will need to let the female incubate them for five to seven days. Then carefully remove the eggs while the parent birds are out of the nest box (this may be a challenge), and hold a light up to the wide end of the egg. If you see red veins inside the egg, it's fertile. If you don't, the egg is clear (infertile). Clear eggs can indicate a number of things, including an incompatible pair, two female birds masquerading as a true pair or illness in the parent birds.

Depending on the species, conure eggs take between 22 and 26 days to incubate. Only the females incubate the eggs during this time. The chicks hatch 24 to 72 hours after they pip, which means that the air space in the wide end of the egg shifts and the chick starts to break out of the shell in search of oxygen.

Newly hatched *Aratinga* chicks have white down and pink skin. Their eyes begin to open about 12 days after they hatch. When the chicks are about 2 weeks old, their legs and beaks begin to darken and the first hint of feather shafts can be seen under their skin. Feather colors begin to appear when the chicks are about 1 month old, and they are fully feathered when they are about 2 months old. At this time, they are also ready to leave the nest. Their parents continue to feed them for several weeks after the chicks leave the nest.

Some *Aratinga* hens become aggressive during breeding season. If your bird becomes aggressive, try to leave her alone as much as possible. Other *Aratinga* hens may bite at or eat their eggs. If you discover your bird has done this, she may need extra calcium, protein or vitamins in her diet.

Recently hatched *Pyrrhura* chicks have pink skin and a hint of down. Their eyes begin to open about two weeks after they hatch, and the chicks show the first signs of feather shafts under the skin when they are about 10 days old. After about 40 days, the chicks are fully feathered and ready to leave the nest, although the male bird continues to feed them for several weeks after they leave the nest.

Bringing Up Babies

Chicks that are still in the nest box can be handled, but be aware that some hens do not appreciate intrusion by humans and will take action, including killing the chicks. This is not a common problem in breeding birds, but it does occur.

Parrot parents become anxious if all the chicks are removed from the nest box at the same time and are kept away from the parent birds for any length of time. This shouldn't discourage you from cleaning the nest box occasionally, but you should make an effort to clean quickly and return the chicks promptly to their parents.

How to Hand-Feed Chicks

Although most parrots are reliable parents, occasionally the need to hand-feed chicks will arise. Some hens will reject chicks, or a hen may die. If you do suddenly find yourself with a nestful of chicks to hand-feed, proper heat and extreme cleanliness are crucial.

Chicks must be kept warm but they should not overheat, so you must strike a delicate balance. Recommended starting points are 85°F for feathered birds and 90°F for unfeathered birds. Adjust the temperature down if the birds start to pant and hold their wings away from their bodies, and adjust up if you see them shivering or huddling together.

Clean hand-feeding supplies and fresh formula will lead to healthier chicks. Keep this in mind if the temptation to cut corners should arise. You should use a different syringe for each baby you feed, and the syringe must be thoroughly cleaned and disinfected between feedings.

Carefully follow the preparation instructions on the package of a good-quality hand-feeding formula. Keep the formula temperature between 100 and 104°F to ensure proper digestion by the chicks. Fill each syringe with the recommended amount of formula (this will vary with the species of bird being fed and the age of the chicks) and place the syringes in a jar of warm, clean water to keep them warm. Get your chicks out of the nest, and place each one in a small, secure container (like an empty margarine tub) with a clean, wadded-up paper towel in the bottom to make cleanup easy.

To hand-feed a chick, put the syringe in the left corner of the bird's mouth and aim the formula in the back right corner of the bird's mouth and throat. Birds have two openings in their throats: One that leads to the lungs (the trachea), located on the left side of the throat, and the other that leads to the stomach (the esophagus), located on the right side of the throat. Obviously, you want the food to go down the esophagus and not into the lungs, where it can cause aspiration pneumonia. Apply firm, gentle pressure to the syringe's plunger and, before you know it, you've hand-fed a bird!

If you take it upon yourself to hand-feed chicks, you must realize that this is a very demanding task. Some chicks will require round-the-clock care, and you must be there to provide it.

Banding Baby Birds

Once your chicks have hatched and are feeding successfully, you will want to band them. Some states require that budgies be banded, and serious breeders want their chicks banded to keep track of bloodlines and successful breeding pairs. Also, bird stores may be reluctant to sell unbanded chicks, so if you plan to do business with a store, you will need to have banded your chicks prior to selling them. You will need to band your chicks when they are about 5 days old. Sometimes you can wait until day 6, but chicks grow quickly, which means you have a very small window of opportunity to get the bands on the chicks!

To band a chick, you will need a clean, dry washcloth to set the chick on during banding, a toothpick and a band (available from parrot clubs or bird supply stores).

Place the chick on the washcloth on a tabletop or other sturdy surface, and turn it onto its right side. Hold the chick's left foot in your left hand and slide the band over the two front toes with your right hand. After you've slipped the band over the first two toes, hold the chick's foot with your right hand and continue moving the band up the chick's leg with your left hand, pulling the toes forward and the band back as you go.

If necessary, use the toothpick to flip the band over the longer back toe. The shorter back toe should follow right along (if not, use your trusty toothpick to gently move the band along), and the chick is banded. Reassure the chick that it's a beautiful, brave bird at this point and return it to the nest.

Chick Development

About four weeks after chicks of smaller species, such as cockatiels or budgies, have been banded, they'll begin to try flying. Be prepared to hear lots of flapping coming from your young birds, and don't be surprised if they first try their wings in their nest box. This will last about a week in most cases, with an adventurous chick finding its way to the nest box opening for its first look at the outside world at the age of 5 weeks. Shortly after, this daring young bird will try its first flight. Make sure to have plenty of perching options available close to the nest box opening because this first flight is traditionally short and weak.

After one chick tests the air, its clutchmates soon follow suit, and breeders are treated to many short, clumsy flights and the chicks' first amusing attempts at perching, side stepping and turning around on the perches. With practice, though, flying, perching, preening and other important skills improve.

Shortly after their first tentative flights into the real world, your chicks should discover the food and water bowls in their parents' cage. By watching their parents crack seeds, sample fresh foods and drink water, the chicks should learn how to eat, but it will probably take them a week or so to perfect their skills. Breeders will enjoy watching their chicks learning to crack seeds because the line between foodstuff and play toy is sometimes quite blurry for a chick! Like any baby, almost anything a parrot chick can get into its mouth is fair game. Keep an eye on curious youngsters so they don't ingest something harmful in these early explorations into the world.

African grey chicks can provide a number of challenges to breeders. Baby greys can be prone to leg and neck problems. Some chicks may be sat on too tightly by their parents, which can result in their leg bones being deformed. This condition is called spraddle leg, and it is not unique to greys. You should consult your avian veterinarian if you notice that your chicks' legs splay out to one side or the other. Splints or even surgery may be needed to correct the problem. A baby with a severely tilted or twisted neck may also be suffering from bacterial or respiratory problems, both of which will require veterinary attention as well.

You may notice that some of your baby greys shake after feeding. Although it may seem that the chick is having convulsions, this behavior is usually not cause for alarm. It often disappears as the babies mature and gain some coordination.

Baby greys' personalities begin to develop when they are about 7 weeks old. They begin by whining for attention and actively seeking affection from their owners. This phase usually passes by the time a bird is weaned (between 12 and 14 weeks of age). Some greys maintain cuddly dispositions, but most become more reserved with age.

Clip a baby grey's wings and nails when it is about 8 weeks of age so it isn't able to fly freely and injure itself or escape and so its nails do not catch on anything as it explores its world. Also, by getting the baby grey used to grooming at an early age, it will accept grooming more readily later on.

When the chicks are about 10 weeks old, they'll begin to try flying. Expect to hear lots of flapping because the chicks will test their wings inside the nest box before actually flying. Baby greys should start sampling grown-up bird food when they are about 12 weeks old.

chapter 8

JUVENILE BEHAVIORS

Young birds have a great many endearing behaviors. They beg for food, they explore nearly everything with their mouths and they are clumsy. Most owners adore their birds at this stage and spend a lot of time cuddling with them and fussing over them.

Some particularly clever birds learn how to exploit their situations by using these behaviors, and owners have to be able to determine when the behaviors are genuine and when a bird is trying to work a situation to its advantage.

Many first-time owners with good intentions create behavioral problems in their baby parrots by spoiling them. Because the chicks are so cute and cuddly and helpless, owners often rush to their baby parrots each time the chick screams. In other cases, the owners hold the birds too much and fail to encourage the bird to spend time by itself. These owners do not teach the baby parrot to entertain itself, so the bird doesn't learn how to play. Finally, some owners spend every waking hour with their birds when the birds are chicks, but then try to engage in other activities once the birds grow up. In all these situations, the potential exists for creating spoiled, uncontrollable feathered monsters.

To keep this from happening to you, offer your baby parrot a balance of cuddling, attention and care from the time you bring it home. Provide it with a safe, secure home, plenty of interesting, nourishing food and lots of clean water. Make sure it has the chance to take naps and get enough sleep (remember, growing up is tiring work!). Take it to the veterinarian regularly to ensure its good health, and keep its nails and wings trimmed for its safety.

Check on your young parrot when it screams to make sure it isn't cold, hungry or in danger, but don't rush to pick it up every time it vocalizes. Instead, occasionally pet the bird on the back and tell it it's a good, brave bird or reward the bird with your attention by playing with it, feeding it a special treat by hand, showing it a new toy or by introducing it to its play gym (be sure your parrot has adequate perching skills before you allow it to sit on a play gym for any length of time).

As your bird grows up, you can reassure its vocalizing from another room with a simple "I'm here. Are you being a good bird?" or some other comment that indicates you have heard the bird's call, but that you aren't going to rush to its side after each vocalization. If the bird continues to vocalize, you may want to check on it to make sure that it did not tip over its food or water bowl, or that it does not have its wing feathers stuck in its cage bars or is in some other uncomfortable situation.

Show your bird around your house when you bring it home, and make sure to take it from room to room regularly. You can give your bird a change of scenery by taking it to look for "pretty birds" in the bathroom mirrors, or you can take your pet on a room-to-room tour of your house in the morning and in the evening so your pet can see other parts of the house, rather than simply sitting in its cage day after day. Offer your bird perching opportunities in different rooms of the house when it is old enough to perch and play safely.

The Weaning Stage

An important part of a young parrot's life is the weaning stage. During weaning, a baby parrot learns to eat solid food rather that the food it receives from its parents or from a hand-feeder. It is a stressful time for both bird and owner as the bird makes the adjustment to an adult diet. Weaning is different from fledging, when a chick starts flying, although some people use the terms interchangeably.

Chicks will often decide for themselves that they no longer want to eat hand-feeding formula, and most will wean between the ages of 5 and 12 weeks. Smaller

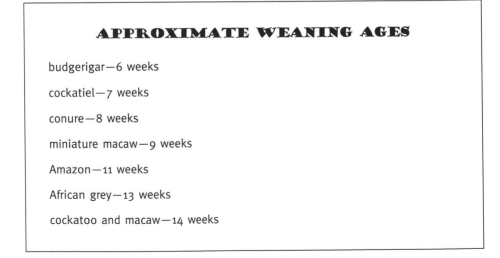

APPROXIMATE WEANING AGES

budgerigar—6 weeks

cockatiel—7 weeks

conure—8 weeks

miniature macaw—9 weeks

Amazon—11 weeks

African grey—13 weeks

cockatoo and macaw—14 weeks

species, such as budgies and cockatiels, wean more quickly than the larger species, such as macaws and cockatoos.

About three weeks before weaning time, start placing small pieces of fruits and vegetables in low-sided bowls in the chick's brooder to encourage it to play with (and hopefully eat) some of these interesting new foodstuffs. Unsweetened cereals are also popular weaning foods. The chick may play with these foods more than it eats them, but at least your pet is being introduced to foods that look, feel and taste differently than the hand-feeding formula that it is used to.

Change the foods frequently because the environment in the brooder will be warmer than your home environment, which may cause food in the brooder to spoil more quickly. Continue to offer feedings of formula if your chick will take them, and monitor your bird's weight carefully. Expect the bird to lose weight—between 10 and 15 percent of its body weight—as it weans. If your bird loses too much weight or seems unable to eat, consult your avian veterinarian or the breeder from whom you bought the bird immediately.

When you start eliminating formula meals for your chick, start by terminating the midday hand-feeding. If the bird seems to be comfortable without its midday meal, try eliminating the morning feeding, too. Offer seeds, pellets and fresh foods during the day to encourage your chick to eat solid food, but still give it an evening feeding of formula so it will have something in its stomach during the night.

Sometimes a chick will wean more easily if it takes its meals of "real food" with you. Offer it its own plate at the table and let it see you and your family eating. If you have other birds in the house, you can enlist them as models of behavior for your chick.

Keep in mind that some chicks in a particular clutch will wean sooner than their clutchmates, and some species, such as cockatoos, wean reluctantly at best.

As parrot chicks grow up in the wild, their parents gradually and gently encourage them to become self-sufficient. Chicks are conditioned from the moment they come out of the egg to beg for food from their parents. They improve their begging skills while their parents are feeding them so that they are true experts by the time they should be weaned. Young parrots in the wild often harass their fathers mercilessly with begging and chasing when they are about to be weaned. However, the parent birds gradually stop giving in to the chicks' begging for food, which forces the chicks to be self-sufficient.

Before the parent birds wean their chicks, they encourage their chicks to explore their surroundings, and many parent birds give their chicks a gentle nudge that gets the young birds started on their first flights. The parent birds continue to encourage their chicks to explore as the chicks are weaned and as they continue to grow. The parent birds teach the chicks where to find food, which foods are good to eat, how to protect themselves against predators and other important life lessons.

In the home environment, parrot owners either don't know or forget to give their young birds gentle nudges toward self-sufficiency. They often make huge fusses over their baby birds when the birds first come into their homes. Couples or family members may compete, in fact, to see who will hold the little bird while it's being hand-fed. As stated earlier, too much attention will discourage the parrot from learning how to entertain itself. As the bird grows up, it's likely to learn to beg for attention, or simply be baffled by the change in its owner's behavior. The stage is set for this poor, confused little parrot to become a screaming, feather-pulling, attention-craving problem pet that may get bounced from home to home. This does not have to happen.

Avian behaviorist Mattie Sue Athan recommends that owners of hand-fed parrots follow these guidelines:

1. Don't continuously hold the newly weaned baby.

2. Reward the bird intermittently when it is entertaining itself in a quiet, successful way.

3. Teach appropriate behaviors, such as the "up" and "down" commands.

4. Keep the bird physically lower than your eyes when in its territory.

5. Provide frequent and varied entertainment that doesn't involve touching and cuddling. This includes music, toys and talking to the bird.

6. Take the bird on outings and encourage interaction with unfamiliar people and objects.

The Terrible Twos

You may have heard the phrase "the terrible twos" used in conjunction with the behavior of young parrots when they are around 1 year old. These behavioral changes can occur any time between the ages of 6 and 30 months, depending on the size of the parrot. Keep in mind that smaller birds mature more quickly than larger ones.

During this period, the parrot will vocalize and explore its territory more than ever before, and it may bite its owner and other humans deliberately. It will also challenge its position in the family, and it may frequently change its loyalties to the people in its family. The person who used to be the parrot's one and only best friend in the whole world may be shunned or chased away in the morning, only to be wooed back by nightfall. This is a very confusing time for the parrot, and it can make owners crazy, too, as the formerly well-behaved little bird seems to turn into a monster before their eyes.

It doesn't have to be this way. Yes, your little feathered friend is changing, but it doesn't have to become a completely unhandleable fiend. If you started your bird on the road to self-sufficiency correctly by teaching it the "up" and "down" commands (see chapter 9) and by encouraging it to play by itself when it was a chick, your adjustment to your parrot's changes will be less stressful than if you had spoiled it as a baby. Still, there will be a period of adjustment as your parrot tries to figure out where it fits in the family flock.

In the wild, this is the time when a young parrot learns about its environment and its flock by exploring its world and testing its independence. It spends time away from its parents, but the young bird also wants to know where they are as it explores. In your home, your young bird will need attention and guidance from you as it explores its new home.

In your flock, your young parrot can test the limits of its environment and find its place in the family's pecking order by climbing, destroying toys and flapping its clipped wings on a play gym or cage top. All these activities help a growing young parrot expend energy and work off its frustrations at growing up.

This period is a perfect time to start teaching your pet to talk. In fact, your bird might surprise you one morning by greeting you with a "Hi!" or a "How ya doin'?" that you didn't even intend to teach it.

This is also the time to offer your pet a wide variety of toy choices. Be sure to introduce each one to your pet carefully because young birds are a bit skittish about new things. By giving your bird several toys at a time, you are allowing it some control over its life by letting it choose the toy it wants to play with. According to avian behaviorist Mattie Sue Athan, the ability to make these choices lets your parrot feel secure when it is presented with new situations in the future.

Many birds enjoy looking at themselves in mirrors. Here Sindbad is playing "find the pretty bird." (Photo by Julie Rach)

Some common household items that can be hazardous to a chewing bird include prescription and over-the-counter medications, matches, pens, pencils, crayons, houseplant fertilizers and chocolate. (PHOTO BY JULIE RACH)

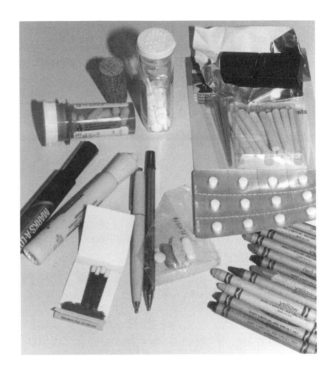

This is also the time to be sure you have parrot-proofed your home because your bird will be exploring every inch of it, and you don't want to tempt your pet into danger, do you? Be aware of these potential dangers in your home:

- unscreened windows and doors, which offer potential escape routes

- mirrors, which can be flown into and cause injury to a bird

- exposed electrical cords, which can cause electrocution if chewed on

- toxic houseplants, which can poison a pet bird

- unattended ashtrays, which can cause burns from lit cigarettes or poisoning from ingesting cigarette butts

- venetian blind cords, in which a bird can hang itself

- sliding glass doors, which can provide an escape route if open or a concussion or broken neck if flown into when closed

- ceiling fans, which can cause broken bones or internal injuries if a bird flies into one while it's on

- open washing machines, dryers, refrigerators, freezers, ovens or dishwashers, which can cause a bird to be injured or killed if the bird flies into it and becomes trapped

- open toilet bowls and uncovered fish tanks, which can cause drowning if fallen into

- leaded stained glass items or inlaid jewelry, which can poison a bird if chewed on

- uncovered cooking pots on the stove, which can cause a variety of injuries, including drowning, scalding or poisoning, particularly by inhaling fumes from overheated nonstick cookware

- crayons and permanent markers, which can poison a bird if chewed on

- pesticides, rodent killers and snail bait, which can poison a bird if eaten

- untended stove burners, which can cause burns when a bird lands on a hot element

- candles, which can burn a bird or poison a pet that chews on them

- sofa cushions, under or between which a parrot can hide

- afghans or balls of yarn, which can entangle a parrot and possibly strangle it

This poor cockatiel fell into a pot of cooking oil. Although it was not burned, the bird still needed immediate veterinary attention so its feathers could be cleaned and so it could be examined for breathing difficulties, potential eye problems, poisoning and shock. (PHOTO BY GARY A. GALLERSTEIN, DVM)

If your bird will spend most of the day by itself, be sure that it has time out of its cage with you in the morning and in the evening, as well as access to interesting toys during the day. (PHOTO BY JULIE RACH)

Take a few minutes to examine your home from your bird's point of view and put tempting items out of reach. By offering your bird a safe environment and appropriate choices about what to chew on, you can help your bird make the transition through "the terrible twos" without it being such a trial for either of you.

As your bird enters this transitional period, be aware that this is the time that some serious behavior problems, such as biting, screaming and feather picking can take root. Frequently, the bird engages in these unwanted behaviors because it discovers that you will give it more attention (yelling at it, shaking your finger or fist at the bird or paying attention to it when it's acting up) if it misbehaves than when it behaves. You have to be careful not to play into your parrot's hand because it will take every opportunity to test you and your patience during this time. Remember that if you've laid the groundwork with your bird by teaching it the "up" and "down" commands and by encouraging it to entertain itself from time to time, you will get through this with your nerves and good humor intact!

If your bird will be spending long periods of time on its own during the day, be sure that it has things to do while you're away. Give your bird interesting foods to eat, challenging toys to play with and a comfortable environment. By leaving on a radio or television set, your bird will have enjoyable background noise. You should also make an effort to spend some time with your bird before you leave the house—perhaps you can have a cup of coffee as your bird is having breakfast in the morning. Soon after you get home in the evening, you can let it out of its cage for a play session.

Juvenile Phobia

If your young bird suddenly displays a fear of absolutely everything, it is having an episode of phobic behavior. Although it will seem as though nothing has changed in your routine, the bird is reacting to changes within its maturing body. It is beginning to feel independent, but if it hasn't been taught how to explore its

Give your bird a change of scenery by allowing it to visit parts of your home outside its cage—it is important to help your bird explore its world safely. (PHOTO BY JULIE RACH)

world safely, it will become phobic and will prefer to stay in its cage all the time because the cage feels safe and secure.

If your bird displays an episode of phobic behavior, all is not lost. You can still help your pet learn how to explore its world safely. Take it to different rooms in your house and talk to it in a positive, upbeat tone. Tell it about its environment, and reassure it that everything will be okay. Make sure your bird has time out of its cage so it doesn't become overly territorial about its cage, or cagebound.

chapter 9

BEHAVIORS EVERY BIRD SHOULD KNOW

Training a parrot takes a great deal of time and patience on the part of the bird owner. You must first gain your pet's trust, and then you must work to never lose it.

A good first step in taming your parrot is getting it to become comfortable around you. To do this, give your bird a bit of warning before you approach its

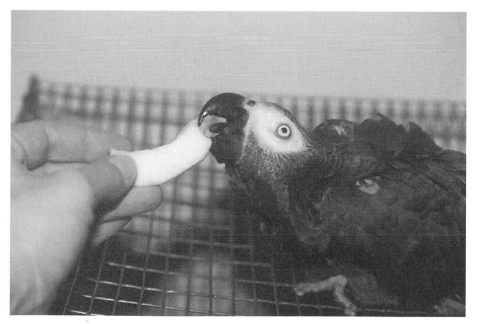

You need to build a bond of trust with your bird in order to successfully train it. Hand-feeding special treats is a good way to reinforce a trusting relationship. (PHOTO BY JULIE RACH)

By teaching the "up" and "down" commands to your bird, you will gain a way to control your pet. (PHOTO BY JULIE RACH)

cage. Don't "sneak up" on your bird, and try not to startle it. Call its name when you walk into the room. Try to be quiet and to move slowly around your pet because these gestures will help it become more comfortable with you. Keep your hands behind you, and reassure the bird that you aren't there to harm it, that everything is all right and that it's a wonderful pet.

After your bird is comfortable having you in the same room with it, you may want to try placing your hand in its cage as a first step toward taking it out of its cage. Place your hand in your bird's cage and hold it there very briefly. Don't be surprised if your bird flutters around and squawks at first at the "intruder."

Continue this process daily, and leave your hand in the cage for slightly longer periods of time each day. Within a few days, your parrot won't make a fuss about your hand being in its space, and it may come over to investigate this new perch. Do not remove your hand from the bird cage the first time your parrot lands on it; just let the bird become accustomed to perching on your hand.

After several successful perching attempts on successive days, try to take your hand out of the cage with your bird on it. Some birds will take to this new adventure willingly, while others are reluctant to leave the safety and security of home. (Be sure your bird's wings are clipped and all doors and windows are secured before taking your bird out of its cage.)

If your bird doesn't seem to respond to this method, you can try an alternate taming method. Take the bird out of its cage and into a small room, such as a bathroom that has been bird-proofed (i.e., the toilet lid is down, the shower door is closed and the bathroom hasn't been recently cleaned with any strong chemical cleansers). Sit down on the floor, place your bird in front of you and begin playing with the bird. Don't be surprised if your bird tries to fly a few times. With

On occasion, parrots need their owners' help to scratch itchy spots that they can't reach. Petting your parrot is a good step to gaining its trust. (PHOTO BY JULIE RACH)

clipped wings, however, it won't get very far and will give up trying after a few failed attempts.

Perching on Your Hand

As your bird becomes more comfortable around you, see if you can make perching on your hand a game for your pet. Once it masters perching on your hand, you can teach it to step up by gently pressing your finger up and into the bird's belly. This will cause the bird to step up. As it does so, say, "Step up" or "Up." Before long, your bird will respond to this command without much prompting. If you aren't comfortable with having your bird climb on your finger, you can use a stick to substitute for your finger during training.

Along with the "up" command, you may want to teach your bird the "down" command. When you put the bird down on its cage or play gym, simply say, "Down," as the bird steps off your hand. These two simple commands offer you a great deal of control over your bird because you can say, "Up," to put an unruly bird back in its cage or you can tell a parrot that needs to go to bed, "Down," as you put the bird in its cage at night.

As you are teaching the "up" and "down" commands, be alert to your bird's moods. If you see what pet owner and author Kevin Murphy describes as the

WHERE TO PET A PARROT

- ears

- nares

- eyelids

- cheeks

- under the wings

- base of the tail

- belly

- wing fold

- under the crest

- under the chin

"aggressive attack posture"—a bird standing tall with wings slightly away from its body and with its neck stretched and beak open—or the "alert wary posture"— the bird digs its nails into your hand tightly, stands tall and holds its wings away from its body—it may be time to stop the sessions. Birds unaccustomed to

Many birds like to be petted on their cheek patches and under their chin.
(PHOTO BY PAMELA L. HIGDON)

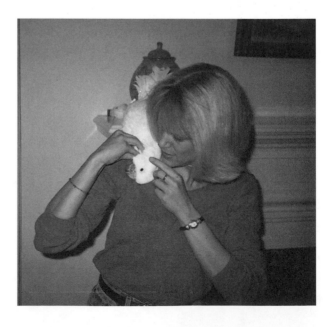

taming sessions will likely show these postures during training, according to Murphy.

When birds are accustomed to being handled, they show a relaxed posture, which has them sitting down to a perching position, lowering their necks and fluffing their feathers. The bird will also be less likely to clutch its owner's hand so tightly with its nails, according to Murphy.

After your bird has mastered the "up" and "down" commands, encourage it to climb a "ladder" by moving it from index finger to index finger (the "rungs"). Keep taming sessions short (about ten minutes is the maximum parrot attention span), and make the taming process fun because it will be much more enjoyable for both of you.

After your pet has become comfortable sitting on your hand, try petting it. Birds seem to like to have their heads, backs, cheek patches, under wing areas and eye areas (including the closed eyelids) scratched or petted lightly. Quite a few like to have a spot low on their backs at the bases of their tails (over their preen glands) rubbed. Many birds do not enjoy having their stomachs scratched, although yours may think this is heaven! You'll have to experiment to see where your bird likes to be petted. You'll know you're successful if your bird clicks or grinds its beak, pins its eyes or settles onto your hand or into your lap with a completely relaxed, blissful expression on its face.

Some people believe that you need to wear gloves while taming your parrot. However, gloves will only make your hands appear more alien, and more frightening, to your bird. If your pet is frightened, it will take more time and patience on your part to tame, which is likely to make the process less enjoyable for you.

Toweling a Parrot

Every parrot should be able to tolerate being wrapped in a towel. Towels make pet birds easier to handle, and they give the birds something to chew on other than an owner's fingers or clothes.

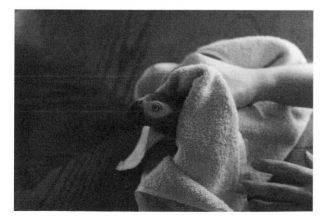

Toweling a parrot can make it easier to handle. Gently grasp your parrot's neck with your toweled hand, and wrap the towel around the wings and body to contain it. Be sure not to constrict the bird's chest in order for it to breathe easily. (PHOTO JULIE RACH)

*To towel a macaw, it is
important to catch the bird
on the ground and in a
corner. You should use a
folded, thick terry cloth
bath towel and keep your
hands behind the towel.*
(PHOTO BY GARY A.
GALLERSTEIN, DVM)

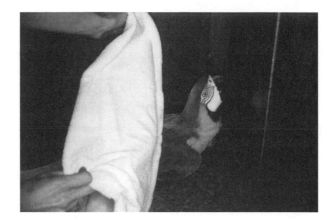

Avian veterinarians often wrap their patients in a towel to handle them, and groomers will towel parrots during wing and nail trimming. If you groom your parrot yourself, you will find the procedure is facilitated if the bird is toweled.

Use a towel appropriate to your bird's size. Budgies, canaries and lovebirds can be toweled with washcloths, and kitchen dish towels work well for medium-sized birds. Bath towels are suitable for larger parrots.

To towel a parrot, you will drape the towel over your hand loosely and reach into your parrot's cage. Catch the parrot's head with your toweled hand and lift the bird off its perch. As you bring the bird out of its cage, support its body with your other hand as you wrap the loose ends of the towel around the parrot's wings and feet, but don't confine the parrot too tightly.

When you've completed the toweling process, your parrot should be secure in the towel, but not wrapped so tightly that it is unable to breathe. Birds need to be able to inhale and exhale easily, and they don't have diaphragms as we do to help them breathe. Keep the towel off your bird's face. Your avian veterinarian can give you a demonstration on how to towel a parrot.

Parrot behavior consultant Mattie Sue Athan reports that parrots show less fear of towels when their owners use towels that are similar in color to that of the parrot. My African grey seems to tolerate gray, black or pastel towels with equal levels of comfort. Any neutral, solid-colored towel should suffice for toweling a parrot. Be sure that the towel you use does not have loose threads hanging off of it—you don't need to have your bird's feet entangled in the towel.

To make toweling easier on your parrot, you can make it a game. Avian behaviorist Sally Blanchard recommends that you play peek-a-boo with a young parrot to make the towel seem less threatening. Move slowly to envelop your parrot loosely in the towel, and reassure it often that it's a brave bird and that toweling is fun!

Parrots can be trained to eliminate on command. Owners need to pay attention to their birds' behaviors to ensure that the birds do not hold their droppings in for long time periods.
(PHOTO BY JULIE RACH)

Housetraining Your Parrot

Although some people don't believe it, parrots can be housetrained so that they don't eliminate on their owners. If you want to housetrain your bird, you will have to choose a word that will indicate the act of eliminating to your pet, such as "go poop" or "go potty." You will have to observe your pet in order to identify how it indicates that it is about to eliminate. Your bird may shift around or squat. When you have mastered your pet's body language, use the chosen phrase at the appropriate time so the bird associates the phrase with the action.

Once your bird seems to associate "go potty" with eliminating, you can try picking it up and holding it until it starts to shift or squat. Tell the bird to "Go potty" while placing it on its cage, where it can defecate. Once it's done, pick it up again and praise it for being such a smart bird! Expect a few accidents while you are both learning this trick, and soon you'll have a housetrained bird. You will be able to set the bird on its cage about every 20 minutes, give it the command and expect the bird to eliminate.

Don't be surprised if your bird occasionally seems to take longer than usual to eliminate. Sometimes my parrot goes right away when I hold her over the trash can, while other times she preens, grooms my bangs, clicks her beak, pins her eyes—in short, doing whatever she can to postpone the inevitable trip back to her cage.

If I try to put her back into her cage after eliminating and she's not ready to go, she will flap her wings furiously as if to make herself larger than the opening of the cage door.

Parrot Tricks

If you have built a good rapport with your parrot and it trusts you, you may be able to teach it some tricks. Some parrots can learn to wave or to roll over, while others can learn to hang upside down from their owner's hand or climb a rope.

If you want to try training your parrot to do tricks, avian behaviorist Christine Davis suggests the following:

Respect the bird's likes and dislikes   If your bird is interested in playing with balls or lying on its back, it's more likely to be a good candidate for learning tricks than one that just likes to sit on your hand and have its head scratched.

Keep training sessions short   Parrots have the attention span of toddlers and, like toddlers, can become cranky if forced to do one thing for too long. Try to limit your training sessions to about ten minutes in length, and when possible, end the session at a time when the bird is performing well. Repeat sessions several times a day.

Keep sessions fun for both of you   If either you or your bird is not having a good time, discontinue the sessions. It is inhumane to starve your pet in order to get it to perform. You can reward good behavior with favored treats, such as sunflower seeds or walnut pieces, but you can also praise your pet and scratch its favorite tickle spots on its body as rewards for performing a trick correctly.

Love your bird for what it is, not for what you want it to be   If, after all your work, your bird just doesn't seem to grasp the concept of the trick you're trying to teach it, don't force the issue. Instead, appreciate your bird for its good points and love it for being your bird buddy.

The extent to which some birds can be trained is illustrated in this account of a parakeet (actually rose-ringed parrots) circus in India. It is taken from Earl Schneider's *All About Parakeets:*

> The trainer repeats the words of instruction almost continuously before the young parrot and helps it in the performance of its task. Though, of course, every concession to the mood and temperament of the bird must be made at the moment, utmost patience is exercised to induce it to do its work.
>
> After a month or two, varying according to the individual capacity of the birds, they learn to listen, understand and execute the performance in obedience to the instructions of their trainer. However, the daily lesson does not last for more than 20 minutes. If this time is exceeded, the bird becomes irritated and tries to run away. The trainer maintains eight to ten of his pets in order to avoid any undue strain on a particular bird, and each is trained only in the one or two numbers of the program of the parrot show. . . . The most interesting item on the program is a motor car accident where a parrot cycling across a road is struck by a motor car driven by another parrot. The injured parrot feigns to be in a serious condition and lies still on the

road side. In the meanwhile the driver runs to the neighboring telephone and sends an urgent call to the doctor. Soon, a third parrot arrives on the scene with his stethoscope, examines the patient and administers a drug out of a vial from the first aid box. The patient recovers his senses, and then the cyclist, the motor car driver and the doctor all go their separate ways, and the show is over amidst the great amusement of the spectators.

Although this elaborate level of training is probably beyond the patience of the average bird owner, it does demonstrate the learning abilities of birds. Some easier tricks you can teach your pet include riding in a wagon, waving, shaking hands or playing dead.

Before you start training a parrot to do tricks, parrot trainer Jennifer Hubbard, author of *The New Parrot Handbook,* suggests that you set up a quiet place for training. In this quiet place, you'll need to have a T-stand for your feathered student, some special treats to reward your bird's behavior, a "bridge" or sound cue that will let your bird know that it has performed a trick correctly (this can be a hand-held clicker or the word "Good!" said in a bright, positive voice) and verbal cues or hand signals to go with the behaviors being taught.

Ride in a Wagon

To teach a bird to ride in a wagon, you must first get it accustomed to the wagon. Roll the wagon in front of your pet to show it what the wagon will do. After a few days of short sessions of watching the wagon roll by, put your bird in the wagon. Praise it and pet it as it sits in the wagon. Let it practice sitting in the wagon for brief periods of time for a few days.

When your bird seems comfortable sitting in the wagon, pull the wagon a short distance. Praise your parrot for its good behavior if it sits calmly, or comfort and reassure it that everything is okay if it seems panicked by the wagon's movement. Put your bird in the wagon for short rides several times a day, and gradually increase the length of those rides.

Wave Hello

To teach your parrot to wave, put your hand out as if you want your bird to step up onto it. When your bird puts out its foot, pet it and praise it lavishly.

After a few sessions of simply having your bird lift its foot, continue the training by stepping away from your bird so that it cannot climb on your hand, but offer your hand just the same. Praise and pet your parrot for raising its foot, and your bird will soon get the idea that you want it to raise its foot.

When your bird has mastered raising its foot at your bidding, raise your hand as you have been, then wave at your parrot. Frequently, it will mimic your actions. Praise and pet it for its ability to follow your lead, and pretty soon, you have a bird that waves!

Some parrots will demonstrate a high level of trust in their owners by learning how to lie on their backs. (PHOTO BY JULIE RACH)

Shake Hands

Shaking hands is a simple extension of the waving gestures. Hold out your hand as if you want the bird to step onto it, and let it take hold of your finger with its foot. Begin shaking the parrot's foot gently. Repeat this series of gestures several times, and soon you have a parrot that shakes hands!

Play Dead

A parrot that likes to be petted and can be turned over by its owner is a good candidate to play dead. First, you must get the bird accustomed to the feel of your hand on its back while it is perching on its cage or play gym. When the bird seems comfortable with your hand on its back, hold it between your hands on its side.

When the bird is accustomed to being held in this way, you can move to holding it between your hands on its back. Once it seems peaceful in this position, remove the hand you have on its feet or belly, and you have a bird playing dead in your hand!

A friend of mine trained her cockatoo to "go to sleep" in this way. She can now flip the bird over in her hand and tell him, "Night-night," to which the bird answers, "Night-night," and closes his eyes. She can then carry him to his cage, where he climbs onto his sleeping perch for the night. She is the only person the bird will allow to do this trick—he doesn't seem to trust anyone else to do it right!

Your bird will have to have an inordinate amount of trust in you before it will allow you to flip it over onto its back. This is not a common parrot posture. Conures are more likely to lie on their backs than other species, but some birds may never be comfortable in this position. If your bird seems distressed when you flip it over on its back, you may have to try to teach it some other trick.

It took me a few years of patient training, but my parrot is now comfortable having me flip her over on her back, and she will lie in my hand this way, and she will lie on her back on the examination table at the veterinarian's office. Inasmuch as she wasn't hand-tamed when I got her, and she didn't even like to be picked up, held or cuddled in her previous home, we have made some progress since we've been together.

I conditioned her to this behavior by flipping her over briefly when I had her out of her cage for her evening cuddle session, and I petted her crop and under her wings and told her she was a very good bird. She didn't really care for being flipped over at first, but she did like having her crop and sides rubbed, so she learned to enjoy being flipped over. I don't keep her on her back for long, which she seems to appreciate, too.

Disciplining Your Parrot

When disciplining your parrot, you must be careful not to lose your temper with your bird and never hit it. Birds are very sensitive, intelligent creatures that do not deserve to be hit, regardless of how angry you are.

Although parrots are clever creatures, they are not linear "cause and effect" thinkers. If a parrot commits action A (chewing on some molding under your kitchen cabinets, for example), it won't associate reaction B (being yelled at, being locked in its cage or being otherwise punished) with the original misbehavior. As a result, most forms of discipline are ineffective with parrots.

So what do you do when your parrot misbehaves? When you must discipline your pet, look at it sternly (what bird behaviorist Sally Blanchard calls "the evil eye") and tell it "No" in a firm voice. If the bird is climbing on or chewing something it shouldn't, remove it from the source of danger and temptation as you tell it "No."

When I discipline my parrot, usually all I have to do is say her name sharply or tell her to "Be quiet" in a firm tone and she gets the message. She often answers my verbal reprimand with an indignant little huff or a series of small squeaks, but she usually settles down after being disciplined verbally. If a verbal reprimand isn't enough, I cover her cage with a dark beach towel for a few minutes to settle her down.

A cage cover can be used to calm a noisy parrot, or it can help a bird settle down for bedtime. (PHOTO BY JULIE RACH)

If your bird has wound itself up into a screaming banshee, sometimes a little "time-out" in its covered cage (between five and ten minutes) does wonders to calm it down. Once the screaming stops and the bird is settled enough to play quietly, eat or simply move around its cage, the cover comes off to reveal a well-behaved, more mellow pet.

On the Road

If you are thinking of traveling with your bird, consider the following issues:

DOES THE BIRD LIKE NEW ADVENTURES?

IS THERE A TRUSTED RELATIVE OR FRIEND THAT YOU CAN LEAVE THE BIRD WITH WHILE YOU ARE AWAY?

DOES YOUR AVIAN VETERINARIAN'S OFFICE OFFER BOARDING?

HOW LONG WILL YOU BE GONE?

IS IT ILLEGAL TO BRING YOUR BIRD TO YOUR DESTINATION?

If you are going on a family vacation, it is usually best to leave the bird at home in familiar surroundings with its own food, water and cage or in the care of a trusted friend, relative, pet-sitter or avian veterinarian.

Generally, travel is stressful for birds because many birds are creatures of habit that like their routines. Moreover, taking birds across state lines or international boundaries is not without risk. It is illegal to bring some species into certain states. For example, California and other states prohibit the entry of Quaker (also known as monk) parrots, on the grounds that the birds are considered a threat to local crops. Some foreign countries have lengthy quarantine stays for pet birds. Although it might be difficult to leave your bird behind, staying at home is usually better for the bird.

These cockatoos are in a suitable cage for traveling, but this cage is too small for these birds to live in full-time. Cockatoos need large cages and plenty of toys to keep their active minds entertained. (PHOTO BY GARY A. GALLERSTEIN, DVM)

Some parrot behavior consultants believe the exact opposite, however; many think travel is a broadening experience for parrots and that it helps them become less territorial and less bonded to their cages and homes. With the advent of pet-friendly superstores, birds have more opportunities to get out and about with their owners than ever before.

Despite my belief that pet birds should stay home, there are still times that they will need to travel, such as when they visit the veterinarian or if you move.

If a car trip is in your pet's future, you will need to acclimate your bird to traveling in the car. Some pet birds take to this new adventure immediately, while others become so stressed out by the trip that they become carsick. Patience and persistence are usually the keys to success if your bird falls into the latter category.

To get your pet used to riding in the car, start by taking its cage (with door and cage tray well secured) out to your car and placing it inside. Make sure that

Car rides can be used to reward birds for good behavior, or they can be used as distractions for pets that like to pick their feathers. (PHOTO BY JULIE RACH)

your car is cool before you do this because your bird can suffer heatstroke if you place it in a hot car and leave it there.

When your bird seems comfortable sitting in its cage in your car, take it for a short drive, such as around the block. If your bird seems to enjoy the ride (it eats, sings, whistles, talks and generally acts like nothing is wrong), then you have a willing traveler on your hands. If it seems distressed by the ride (it sits on the floor of its cage shaking, screams or vomits), you have a bit of work ahead.

Distressed birds often need only to be conditioned to traveling in the car. You can do this by talking to your bird throughout the trip. Praise it for good behavior and reassure it that everything will be fine. Offer special treats and juicy fruits (grapes, apples or citrus fruit) so your pet will eat and will also take in water. (On long trips, you may want to remove your pet's water dish during travel to avoid spillage. If you do take out the dish, make sure to stop frequently and give your bird water so it doesn't dehydrate.)

As your bird becomes accustomed to car travel, gradually increase the length of the trips. When your bird is comfortable with car rides, begin to prepare it for the trip by packing your car as you would on the first travel day. If, for example, you plan to place duffel bags near your bird's cage, put the bags and the cage in the back of the car for a "practice run" before you actually begin the trip so your bird can adjust to the size, shape and color of the bags. A little planning on your part will result in a well-adjusted avian traveler and a reduced stress level for you both.

My parrot enjoys car trips immensely. When we first began traveling together, I would put her cage on the front passenger seat of my car so she could see me and I could talk to her during the trip. She could climb up into the corner of her cage closest to me and hang on to the cage bars, watching me drive, whistling her own tunes to accompany the music from the radio, grinding or clicking her beak and pinning her eyes at me. I think she also enjoys the feeling of the air-conditioning blowing through her feathers because she made sure to position herself so that the vents could blow on her full force, even on only slightly warm days. However, after giving the matter some thought, I believe she is safer riding in the back seat of my compact sedan, so that's where she has traveled for the past five years. I try to place her cage behind the passenger seat so she can still see me and I can keep an eye on her, too.

You may be tempted to have your pet ride in your car without being confined to its cage. You may have seen pictures of birds perched on car headrests in magazines or been intrigued by the concept of an avian car seat. Please resist these temptations because your bird could easily fly out of an open car window or be injured severely in the event of an accident if it is not in a secure carrier or cage while traveling in your car.

chapter 10

MANAGING UNDESIRABLE BEHAVIORS

Parrots are wonderful pets, but they do have some behaviors that owners find puzzling, troubling or downright dangerous. These behaviors include biting, chewing, screaming, feather pulling, self-mutilation, excessive egg laying and dominance. In many cases, these behaviors make perfect sense to the parrot, but they can frustrate even the most patient and understanding parrot owner. The good news is that many of them can be managed effectively or even prevented completely.

Although parrots are tame, parrots are not domesticated to the same degree as dogs and cats. Some captive-bred parrots are only a few generations away from life in the jungle, and people whose parrots were originally wild-caught essentially have a tame wild animal living with them. Part of the parrot's initial appeal and charm to its new owner is the bird's independent nature, but it's that same nature that often causes friction between pet and owner, particularly as the pet matures.

Avoid Instigating Problem Behaviors

In some cases, owners cause their birds to behave in inappropriate ways. For example, an Amazon owner who is roughhousing with his parrot shouldn't be surprised that the bird gets excited and bites him while in the throes of emotional overload, but the owner gets both his hand and his feelings hurt when he is nipped by his pet. In another case, an African grey owner who is playing with her bird's beak stimulates the bird to begin regurgitating its last meal to her. In still another instance, an evening cuddle with a male cockatoo by his owner causes him to initiate breeding behaviors, including displays and masturbation.

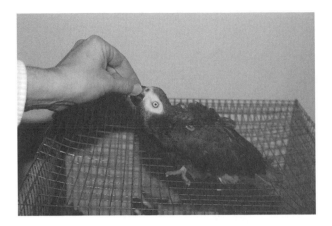

Beak wrestling can be viewed as a greeting, as a challenge to fight or as a prelude to mating. An owner who plays with his or her bird's beak could be setting the bird up to bite. (PHOTO BY JULIE RACH)

In all of these situations, the birds are exhibiting normal, natural reactions to the stimuli presented by their owners. It's the owners' perceptions of how their birds should behave that are the problems, and certainly the owners' behavior that needs to be modified to prevent these situations from occurring again.

When your parrot misbehaves, rather than getting angry at it, take a moment to see what caused the bird to misbehave. Parrots are not just "dumb animals" that misbehave for no reason, and often the behavior is motivated by something the owners have done or a factor in the environment. Did your bird bite you because you provoked it with frightening body language, or did a large bird just swoop by your sliding glass door? Did your bird scream because it saw a squirrel on the balcony that needed to be chased away, or did you cause the bird to scream by "abandoning" it?

By taking a moment to see what your bird's motivation for misbehavior is, you can often prevent the problem from recurring.

Many cases of apparent parrot misbehavior are really a reflection of misguided owners. Their expectations are too high, or they want their parrot to be something it cannot be. Bonnie Munro Doane and Thomas Qualkinbush put it very well in their book, *My Parrot, My Friend,* when they said:

> To live happily with a parrot requires patience and tolerance for behavior that is normal to the bird. Acceptance of a certain amount of mess, noise and destruction of property will go a long way in preventing the development of relationship difficulties between person and parrot. If the parrot has been properly socialized, its natural tendencies to boisterousness and self expression should not be unpleasant for the owner. Occasionally "accidents" will happen, as they do with small children. But they should be the exception, not the rule. As long as the owner understands that there is no such thing as perfection with a parrot, the parrot/owner relationship should be mutually pleasant and satisfying.

Birds that bite have often learned this behavior as a response to the behavior of their owners. (PHOTO BY PAMELA L. HIGDON)

Some unpleasant behaviors can become more than an annoyance, and correction is essential for a happy relationship between bird and owner.

Biting

Getting bitten by your pet parrot hurts, and if you happen to have a large bird, such as a macaw or a cockatoo, the potential exists for serious injury.

Biting is not a natural behavior in the wild, according to parrot behavior consultant Liz Wilson. In their native habitats, parrots use their beaks to climb, eat, wrestle or preen, but they rarely bite one another. If a parrot in the wild wants to intimidate an opponent, it's likely to scream, strut, posture or fluff feathers to look larger, rather than resort to biting. If a bird does bite another bird, it is likely to get nothing more than a mouthful of feathers.

According to Wilson, birds in captivity bite for one of two reasons: survival or control. Survival biting often occurs when a bird is terribly frightened or it is injured. Control biting means that a parrot is given some kind of reward that encourages it to bite again. Remember, yelling, cursing or shaking your bitten hand in the air does not feel like "positive reinforcement" to you, but, rest assured, your parrot likes it!

According to avian behaviorist Mattie Sue Athan, several instinctive behaviors may cause a bird to bite the first time, including crankiness, territorialism and sexual-related aggression. Add in provocative behavior on the part of people,

PROBLEM BEHAVIORS AT A GLANCE

Why does my bird scream?

- the bird is stressed about or afraid of something in its environment
- the bird is reflecting some stress felt by its owner
- the bird's owner has rewarded the bird for screaming in the past
- the bird learned how to scream from another bird
- screaming feels good
- the bird is tired
- the bird is being fed an all-seed diet
- the bird is protecting its flock and family
- the bird is sexually mature and wants to breed
- the bird does not know how to entertain itself
- the bird is hungry or thirsty and has run out of food or water
- the bird needs more exercise
- the bird feels isolated from its family

What can I do to prevent it from screaming?

- check to make sure the bird isn't in danger, then reassure it that it's okay
- offer the bird opportunities to interact regularly with its owner or family
- let the bird out of its cage for daily exercise and playtimes
- make sure the bird has ample opportunities to sleep
- feed the bird a balanced diet
- offer your bird a combination of care, guidance and discipline

- don't reward the bird for screaming by yelling at it, storming into its room or shaking your finger or fist at it

Why does my bird bite?

- it is afraid
- you are rushing the bird through its usual routine
- it is overstimulated by you
- the bird is being fed an all-seed diet
- it is a baby that is exploring its environment
- it is trying to get its "mate" to flee from a perceived threat
- it wants to be the dominant creature in its relationship with you

What can I do to prevent it from biting?

- avoid roughhousing with your bird because you may excite it and cause it to bite
- offer your bird safe opportunities to explore its environment
- offer your bird a variety of interesting toys and foods to chew on
- slow down when you're interacting with your bird
- don't reward the bird for biting by pulling your hand away each time it reaches out to you you

Why does my bird pull its feathers?

- the bird has a physical problem, such as a *Giardia* infestation, psittacine beak and feather disease syndrome, thyroid deficiency or an infection

- the bird is stressed by something in its environment
- the bird is nervous
- the bird has been rewarded with attention by its owner when it pulls its feathers
- the bird is sexually frustrated
- the humidity in the bird's environment is too low
- the bird is being fed an all-seed diet
- the bird is bored
- the bird learned how to pull its feathers from another bird

What can I do to prevent it from pulling its feathers?

- take the bird to your avian veterinarian for an evaluation
- look at your bird's environment to see what's causing it to feel stress
- offer your bird a varied diet
- offer your bird many interesting chew toys
- play with your bird regularly
- set up a comfortable routine for your bird
- don't reward it for pulling its feathers with extra attention

Why does my bird refuse to talk?

- the bird has yet to learn to talk
- poor education—too many people are trying to teach the bird to talk or too many phrases are being taught at the same time
- the bird doesn't feel well physically
- something in the bird's environment is causing it to feel uncomfortable

How can I get my bird to talk?

- keep training sessions short
- start with one phrase and stick to it
- be positive and upbeat in the training sessions
- be patient

Why does my bird throw up?

- it is regurgitating food to show affection for its chosen human
- something has frightened it
- it has a crop infection and needs medical attention
- it has a blockage in its digestive tract and needs medical attention

How can I help it to stop throwing up?

- be careful how you pet your bird, particularly its beak
- have your bird evaluated by an avian veterinarian if it shows other signs of illness

Why does my bird get quiet around strangers?

- having strangers around frightens your parrot

How can I help it be more comfortable around strangers?

- introduce your bird to new people and places early in its life
- have more than one person handle your bird regularly
- have more than one person be responsible for daily bird care

unintentional reinforcement and misunderstanding of how a bird uses its beak and, *voilà!* you have a biting parrot.

If your parrot bites you while it's perched on your hand or if it begins chewing on your clothing or jewelry, you can often dissuade it from this behavior by gently rotating your wrist about a quarter turn. Your bird will quickly associate the rocking of its "perch" with its misbehavior and will stop biting or chewing. Don't rock your arm if you have a young parrot on your arm, however. Young birds are unsteady on their feet, and a rocking arm could shake their confidence greatly. Some behaviorists recommend ignoring initial nips from baby birds because in many cases the birds are just trying to maintain their balance the only way they know how.

If your bird bites you, do not thump it on its beak as punishment. It's easy to react to your bird's behavior with a quick thump on the beak, and it was a gesture encouraged by some bird tamers who worked with wild-caught parrots. However, parrot behavior consultants have since discovered that birds do not understand this kind of punishment, and such a gesture will encourage your bird to want to bite you that much harder the next time it gets a chance.

Similarly, don't grab your bird's beak to discipline it. Grabbing a bird's beak can say several things to a bird: It can be a greeting, it can indicate sexual behavior or it can issue a challenge to fight to a pet bird. If your bird enjoys having its beak touched and gently wrestled with, you can reward it with these gestures, but don't try this as a form of discipline. Your parrot will not perceive it as punishment.

To prevent your bird from biting, make sure it has access to plenty of acceptable chew toys, an interesting variety of foods and opportunities to exercise outside its cage.

Don't encourage your bird to bite by pulling your hand away when your bird tries to test the strength of the perch you're offering. Very clever parrots soon learn to intimidate people in this way, and they quickly become biters. In other cases, birds learn to bite if their owners offer toys or treats each time the bird reaches out toward its owner's hands or clothing with its beak.

Bird bites tend to hurt more than a finger or hand: They also hurt the bird owner's feelings. I've heard people say things such as, "My bird must not like me any more because he bit me," or, "Why did my bird turn on me? I hand-raised her." Although birds are intelligent creatures capable of a wide range of emotions, they don't equate liking or not liking a person with their ability to bite this person.

Frequently, the bird really does like the person it bit and is showing its affection in this way. If a bird owner is bitten on the face, the bird may have been trying to encourage the person to flee from some perceived danger. (Birds relate most closely to our faces—they don't seem to know quite what to do with the rest of us.) In other cases, the bird is expressing its hormonal surges or feelings of frustration at being unable to breed.

You are well advised not to take a bird bite personally. This is a normal part of bird ownership that's to be expected. You can take some steps to minimize your chances of being bitten (for example, by exercising caution when handling a sexually mature parrot during breeding season), but you cannot realistically eliminate biting from your parrot's repertoire of behaviors.

Don't stop handling a bird that bites because a lack of physical contact could create additional problems and result in a relationship that neither you nor your bird enjoys very much. A parrot that is never handled or played with will be "in control," but is also likely to become phobic. It may become overly attached to its cage, or cagebound, which makes it even more prone to bite because it feels compelled to defend its territory. In addition, the parrot feels neglected and may start other behavioral problems, such as feather picking or screaming, while the owner feels hurt and unloved by the bird.

Avoid this problem by offering your bird consistent discipline and guidance from the time you bring it home. Also pay attention to your pet's body language and the signals it sends out. Often, a bird gives plenty of warning before it bites—as long as you know how to interpret its body language.

If your bird has started to become cagebound, you must take steps to prevent it from becoming increasingly attached to its home. Take the bird out of its cage and take it into another room in your home—a room that is not as familiar to the bird as the room its cage is in. Play with the bird in this room and teach it (or give it a refresher course in) the "up" and "down" commands. Let the bird explore this new room and other rooms in your house in the course of your play sessions.

When you return your bird to its cage, give it another refresher session in the "up" and "down" commands before putting it back in its cage. After a few play sessions away from its cage and diligent work with the "up" and "down" commands,

---

WHAT'S LOVE GOT TO DO WITH IT?

You can foster a good relationship with your bird by remembering that a parrot does not love its owner in the same way humans love one another. Yes, parrots demonstrate emotion, and yes, they do become attached to their owners, but love may be too anthropomorphic an emotion to credit to your pet bird. You'll have an easier time accepting your parrot's occasional episodes of misbehavior if you keep in mind that it is not trying to "break up" with you. Some of these behaviors are caused by hormonal surges that your pet bird cannot control.

you should be able to handle your formerly cagebound bird with ease. Again, remember to watch your pet for signs that it wants to bite you, and take steps to prevent this from happening. You can still enjoy your pet, even when it's sexually mature, if you use a little common sense.

Chewing

Parrots chew to keep their beaks in condition. Chewing becomes a problem behavior in pet situations when the owner does not provide ample opportunity for a parrot to chew on acceptable items. The bird then turns its chewing needs loose on whatever it can find, such as furniture, wallpaper or paneling.

Bird owners can prevent episodes of problem chewing simply by anticipating a bird's need to chew and providing acceptable items for this purpose. These can include wooden or leather toys, cardboard rolls from paper towels, toilet paper rolls or nuts in the shell. Some birds are wild about chewing on seemingly indestructible things, such as manzanita perches or Plexiglas toys. You may want to save some of your bird's favorite kinds of chew toys to use as a distraction when it seems determined to chew on anything it can get its beak on.

Although it may seem incredibly simple, you can control a parrot's chewing tendencies by limiting its access to chewables in the home. In addition to

Your parrot won't know the difference between your jewelry and acceptable chew toys. It's up to you to provide your pet with appropriate things to chew on. (PHOTO BY JULIE RACH)

stringent housekeeping, you will need to supervise your bird when it's out of its cage. If your bird can't get its beak on your antiques, your answering machine or your prized houseplants, it can't chew on any of these items, now can it?

Screaming

Screaming is another behavior that makes perfect sense to a parrot but may cause an owner to wonder why he or she didn't adopt a nice quiet hamster instead of a bird.

All parrots will make noise during the day. They often greet the dawn and say goodnight to the sun by being especially vocal early in the morning or late in the day. This is normal psittacine behavior that can be curbed somewhat but not completely eliminated.

Sometimes parrots are just a little lonesome and in need of reassurance, so they scream to see where their people are. In these cases, simply call back to your bird with an "I'm here. Are you okay?" or another reassuring phrase. In many cases, the bird will quiet down quickly after hearing your voice.

In other cases, a bird screams because it feels isolated from its family. My own bird demonstrated this conduct. I put her cage on the far side of the living room, thinking that she would benefit from the sunshine and the view afforded by the patio door on that side of the room. However, she screamed almost every night around suppertime. I thought she was saying good night to the sun, that she was hungry or tired, and I really didn't think much more about it.

An infestation of ants made it necessary to move her cage away from the patio door and about 10 feet closer to the dining room and kitchen area in my town house. I sprayed the area with Camicide, and I moved her cage to make spraying safer for her and easier for me.

Originally, I had planned to make the move temporary, but she was so much quieter and seemed so much more content in the new location that I left her alone. I believe she felt she was too far away from the center of activity (the dining room table) and was letting me know that by screaming.

At other times, birds may scream because something in the environment frightens them. In these cases, you will have to work with the bird over time to desensitize it to whatever it finds scary. If your bird screams at you when you wear a hat, for example, set the hat on a table far away from the bird's cage and gradually (over a period of a few days or a week), bring the hat closer to your bird's cage. Tell your bird how brave it is as the hat gets closer to the cage, and cuddle it and pet it to further reward its bravery.

Still other birds scream because they think they have to "protect" their home and families. This type of vocalizing clearly hearkens back to the wild, where parrots alert each other to danger in the area by screaming or calling to one another. In these cases, it's a good idea to check to see that your toaster isn't smoking or

Screaming, a normal parrot behavior, can easily get out of control. (PHOTO BY JULIE RACH)

there isn't a crow perched on the balcony railing before disciplining your helpful watch-parrot.

Other birds will scream when they are tired. In these cases, covering the cage for a few minutes will invariably have a soothing effect. If your bird seems to be consistently tired and cranky, you may have to adjust its bedtime. Remember that birds need about 12 hours of sleep a night. If your bird is in the living room with you as you watch television or as your children do homework under a bright desk lamp, its natural sleep rhythms may be disturbed. You may ease the situation by providing a heavier cage cover or by relocating the bird to another part of the house. But remember—don't banish your bird to some far-flung, seldom-used part of your house because feelings of neglect or isolation can also cause screaming.

Some screaming birds learn how to scream from other parrots in the home. If you have one screaming bird in your flock, don't be surprised if other birds adopt the behavior, especially if you reward the screaming bird by making large outbursts of emotion whenever it screams. Birds love this stuff and will do whatever they can to receive more of this kind of attention!

If your bird likes to scream, you may be able to train it to whistle or say "hello" instead of screaming. To do this, you'll have to whistle or say whatever you want the bird to say in response to the screaming. Reward your parrot with attention when it whistles back or repeats the phrase you're trying to teach it, and ignore it when it screams in response to you. Your bird should quickly catch on to what you want it to do, and you'll have resolved the screaming problem!

Once again, the fundamentals of good care will help to prevent or alleviate problem screaming. Give your bird consistent attention (at least two hours a day); allow it ample opportunities to exercise outside of its cage by flapping or climbing; provide it with an interesting environment, complete with a variety of toys and a well-balanced diet; and leave a radio or television on when you're away to provide background noise. If you treat your bird right, it shouldn't become a screamer.

Other Problem Behaviors

Feather picking, self-mutilation, egg laying and dominance are all behaviors that cause problems for parrots and their owners. As I've said in other parts of the book, many things can cause a bird to pull its feathers or mutilate itself, including illness, boredom, stress and the desire to breed. The desire to breed may also cause a female bird to lay eggs, and some species may be prone to laying large number of eggs during breeding season. I have heard reports of cockatiels that lay more than 20 eggs in a single season.

Some birds have been encouraged by their owners to be dominant because the birds have unlimited access to their owners' shoulders or to high places in the home, or they live in large, tall cages that allow them to frequently have their heads higher than their owners.

When setting up their birds' homes, owners need to remember that height is power in the parrot world. If your bird's cage allows it to be taller than most family members when it is atop the cage, you may want to lower the cage height slightly or provide steps or other means for shorter family members to gain height when dealing with your bird. Make sure to hold and carry your parrot at mid-chest height to allow you some control over your parrot and its behavior.

Patience Is a Must

Although you want to solve your bird's behavior problems promptly, don't settle for quick-fix solutions, such as putting the bird in a dark closet or spraying it in the face with water. Remember that birds don't think in "cause and effect" terms, so they won't understand why you are punishing them. Such quick fixes will actually do more damage to the long-term relationship you have with your pet, which could lead to even more behavior problems in the future. You can't resolve your bird's problem behaviors without taking the time to learn the cause or causes.

Moreover, your bird's misbehavior probably didn't start overnight, so why should you expect an instant solution to the problem? It would be nice if things worked that way, but unfortunately, they don't.

Drug Therapy

In extreme cases of psittacine behavior problems that cannot be resolved through behavior modification, an avian veterinarian may prescribe psychotropic (or mood-altering) drugs. Some cases of feather picking or self-mutilation have been successfully treated using these drugs.

If your avian veterinarian recommends drug therapy for your parrot, you must still continue with behavior modification methods, such as offering toys, playing with your bird or varying its diet. In addition to the behavior modification, you will need to watch your parrot closely to see that the drugs are helping to stop your parrot's behavior problems. You must also be alert for signs of side effects because these drugs can cause liver and kidney problems in pet birds.

Two types of drug therapy have shown promise in alleviating behavior problems in pet birds: traditional medications and holistic treatments. Common medications used in parrots with behavior problems include Valium, Elavil, Anafranil and Haldol. Potential side effects of these medications include drowsiness, lethargy, thyroid problems, kidney problems, increased appetite and water consumption and tremors. Holistic products that have shown some promise include belladonna, nux vomica, arnica and nat mur. Consult your veterinarian before giving your bird any medications.

Drug therapy is not a behavioral modification step that should be taken lightly or quickly. Discuss drug therapy options fully with your avian veterinarian. The two of you know the status of your bird's health and which options you have explored regarding behavioral modification. Together, you can make the best decision for your pet.

chapter 11

WILL MY BIRD TALK?

A bird's ability to talk has been one of the most appealing aspects of pet bird ownership since the days of the ancient Romans. A description of parrots written by the Greek historian and physician Ctesias tells of the talking ability of a parrot he called *Bittacus,* which experts now believe was a plum-headed parakeet. This bird could speak both Greek and an Indian language.

Some species are more prone to talking than others. African greys, Amazons, budgerigars and mynahs are considered among the best talking birds, but none of them is guaranteed to talk. With persistence and patience on the owner's part, a bird from a species not noted for talking may learn a few words or even a few phrases.

Three parrots have amassed particularly noteworthy vocabularies. Puck, a budgie in northern California, holds the Guinness World Record for largest vocabulary by an animal. Puck's owner estimates that her bird has a 1,728-word vocabulary! Another parrot, an African grey named Prudle, reportedly had a 1,000-word vocabulary when he retired from public life in 1977.

Sparkie, a budgie that lived in Great Britain from 1954 to 1962, held the record for a talking bird in his time. He won the BBC's Cage Word Contest in 1958 by reciting eight four-line nursery rhymes without stopping. At the time of his death, Sparkie had a vocabulary of 531 words and 383 sentences.

Sometimes, a parrot will surprise you with its ability to say just the right thing at just the right time. While watching a movie one night, my bird surprised me by saying "Good-bye!" in a rather loud voice to one of the characters in the film as he exited a scene. Another parrot I know yells, "Night-night!" to get slow-moving dinner guests out the door so he can go to bed.

SPECIES MOST LIKELY TO TALK

African greys   Amazons   Budgerigars   Mynahs

The tips offered below will help you teach your pet bird to talk, but please don't be disappointed if your pet never utters a word.

You may notice that your parrot is more vocal early in the morning or at dusk. Your bird may be more receptive to speech lessons at these times of day.

Remember that language, whether it's bird or human, helps members of a species or group communicate. Most baby birds learn the language of their parents because it helps them communicate within their family and their flock. A pet bird raised with people may learn to imitate the sounds it hears its human family make, but if you have more than one bird, the birds may find communicating with each other easier and seemingly more enjoyable than trying to learn your language.

Although most birds raised around humans do learn to talk, some choose to make other sounds. Calvin, a physically challenged budgerigar I used to bird-sit,

You will be more successful in training a bird to talk if you keep a single pet. Birds kept in groups are more likely to bond with one another and to speak "Birdese" rather than to bond with humans and learn to speak our language. (PHOTO BY GARY A. GALLERSTEIN, DVM)

had ample opportunity to learn human speech from his owner and other people who saw him regularly in her office. Instead of speaking English, though, Calvin chose to imitate the computer printer, modem and other machines found in his owner's office!

You will be more successful in training a bird to talk if you keep a single pet, rather than a pair. Birds kept in pairs or groups are more likely to bond with other birds than to bond with people. By the same token, don't give your bird any toys with mirrors on them if you want the bird to learn to talk, as your bird will think that the bird in the mirror is a potential cagemate with whom it can bond.

It is best to start speech training with a young bird because younger birds are more likely to want to mimic human speech. It is also best to start with one phrase. Keep it short and simple, such as the bird's name. Say the phrase slowly so the bird learns it clearly. Some people teach their birds to talk by rattling off words and phrases quickly, only to be disappointed when the bird repeats them in a blurred jumble that cannot be understood.

Be sure to say the chosen phrase with emphasis and enthusiasm. Birds like a "drama reward" and seem to learn words that are said emphatically, which may be why some of them pick up bad language so quickly! Make sure to watch your language around your bird, or you may be surprised to find out that it learns words you had no intention of teaching it!

If you want to teach your bird to talk, start with one phrase and make sure that you have the bird's attention. Train your bird in a quiet place, speak positively and keep the training sessions short. (PHOTO BY PAMELA L. HIGDON)

Try to have phrases make sense. For example, say "Good morning" or "Hello" when you uncover the bird's cage each day. Say "Good-bye" when you leave the room, or ask "Want a treat?" when you offer your pet its meals. Phrases that make sense are also more likely to be used by you and other members of your family when conversing with your bird. The more your bird hears an interesting word or phrase, the more likely it is to say that phrase someday.

Don't change the phrase. If you're teaching your bird to say "Hello," for example, don't say "Hello" one day, then "Hi" the next, followed by "Hi Petey!" (or whatever your bird's name is) another day.

Keep training sessions short. Ten- to 15-minute sessions seem to be the time frame recommended by most bird behavior experts.

Train your bird in a quiet area. Think of how distracting it is when someone is trying to talk to you with a radio or television blaring in the background. It's hard to hear what the other person is saying under those conditions, isn't it? Your bird won't be able to hear you any better or understand what you are trying to accomplish if you try to train it in the midst of noisy distractions. Be sure to keep your bird involved in your family's routine, though, because isolating it completely won't help it feel comfortable and part of the family. Remember that a bird needs to feel comfortable in its environment before it will draw attention to itself by talking.

Be patient with your pet. Stop the sessions if you find that you are getting frustrated. Your bird will sense that something is bothering you and will react by becoming bothered itself. This is not an ideal teaching and learning environment. Try to keep your mood upbeat. Smile a lot and praise your pet when it does well!

Graduate to more difficult phrases as your bird masters simple words and phrases. Consider keeping a log of the words your bird knows (this is especially helpful if more than one person will be teaching your pet to talk).

When you aren't talking to your pet, try listening to it. On occasion, birds mumble to themselves to practice talking as they drift off to sleep. Because some birds have very small voices, you'll have to listen carefully to see if your pet is making progress.

You may be curious about the efficacy of the talking tapes and compact discs sold in pet stores and through advertisements in bird magazines. Some birds do learn from the repetition of the tapes and CDs that, fortunately, have gotten livelier and more interesting to listen to in recent years. Other birds benefit from having their owners make tapes of the phrases the bird is currently learning and hearing those tapes play when their owners aren't around. I would not recommend playing taped phrases for your bird during the day. The repetition is likely to bore your bird, and if it's bored, the bird will be more likely to tune out the tape and tune out the training in the process.

Finally, if your consistent, patient training seems to result in no progress, you may have to accept the fact that your bird isn't going to talk. We finally had to do this with my childhood pet, Charlie. Despite my mother's most patient attempts to teach the bird to say "Pretty bird," he never learned to talk. My mother did things by the book, too. Charlie was a budgie, which meant he was more likely to talk than other psittacine species. My mother spoke in a bright, cheerful voice, she kept the training sessions short, she kept a positive attitude and tone when talking to the bird and she displayed patience that rivaled Job's, but Charlie remained silent. Perhaps he was too old, perhaps he was too isolated or perhaps he just wasn't interested in the phrase.

As I've said before, don't be too disappointed if your pet doesn't learn to talk. As one *Bird Talk* reader stated, "Talking should be the icing on the cake," rather than the primary reason for owning a bird. If your pet never learns to talk, continue to love it for the unique creature that it is, rather than what you want it to be.

chapter 12

BEHAVIORS EVERY BIRD OWNER SHOULD KNOW

Bird keeping isn't particularly difficult to do. In fact, if you only do ten things for your bird for as long as you own it, your bird should have a healthy, well-adjusted life.

The Ten Commandments of Bird Care

First, provide a safe, secure cage that is appropriate for your bird's size in a secure, yet active, location in your home.

Next, clean the cage regularly to protect your pet from illness and to make its surroundings more enjoyable for both of you.

Third, clip your bird's wings regularly to ensure its safety. Bird-proof your home and practice bird safety by closing windows and doors securely before you let your bird out of its cage, keeping your bird indoors when it isn't caged and

By closing windows and doors before letting your bird out of its cage, and by keeping its wings clipped, you protect your pet from an undesired escape.
(PHOTO BY JERRY THORNTON)

ensuring that your pet doesn't chew on anything harmful or become poisoned by toxic fumes from overheated nonstick cookware, cleaning products and other household products.

Fourth, offer your pet a varied diet that includes seeds or pellets (if your pet is a parrot, canary or finch), nectar (if it's a softbill), fresh vegetables and fruits cut into appropriate-sized portions and healthy people food. Provide the freshest food possible, and remove partially eaten or discarded food from the cage before it has a chance to spoil. Your bird should also have access to clean, fresh drinking water at all times.

Next, establish a good working relationship with a qualified avian veterinarian early on in your bird ownership (preferably on your way home from the pet store or breeder). Don't wait for an emergency to locate a veterinarian.

Sixth, take your pet to the veterinarian for regular checkups, as well as when you notice a change in its routine. Illnesses in birds are often difficult to detect before it's too late to save the bird, so preventive care is a must.

Seventh, set and maintain a routine for your bird. Make sure that your bird is fed at about the same time each day, that its playtime out of its cage occurs regularly and that its bedtime is well established.

Eighth, provide an interesting environment for your bird. Make it feel that it's part of your family. Entertain and challenge your bird's curiosity with a variety of safe toys. Rotate these toys in and out of your bird's cage regularly, and discard any that become soiled, broken, frayed, worn or otherwise unsafe.

Ninth, leave a radio or television on for your bird when you are away from home because a too-quiet environment can be stressful for many birds, and stress can cause illness or other problems for your pet.

Finally, pay attention to your pet on a consistent basis. Don't lavish abundant attention on the bird when you first bring it home, then gradually lose interest in it. Birds are sensitive, intelligent creatures that will not understand such a mixed message. Set aside a portion of each day to pay attention to your bird—you'll both

Change the toys in your bird's cage regularly to keep your pet's environment interesting. (PHOTO BY JULIE RACH)

enjoy it, and your relationship will benefit from it. Besides, wasn't companionship one of the things you were looking for when you picked a bird as a pet?

A Daily Care Routine

Along with daily attention from and interaction with you, its owner, your bird requires a certain level of care each day to ensure its health and well-being. Here are some of the things you'll need to do each day for your pet:

Observe your bird for any changes in its routine (report any changes to your avian veterinarian immediately).

Offer fresh food and water and remove old food and water bowls. Wash dishes thoroughly with detergent and water. Rinse completely and allow to dry.

Provide fresh paper in the cage tray.

You'll want to cover your bird's cage at about the same time every night to indicate bedtime. All pet birds seem to enjoy a familiar routine. When you cover the cage, you'll probably hear your bird rustling around for a bit, perhaps getting a drink of water or a last mouthful of food before settling in for the night. Keep in mind that your pet will require eight to ten hours of sleep a day, but you can expect that it will take naps during the day to supplement its nightly snooze.

Although it may seem a bit unpleasant to discuss, your bird's droppings require daily monitoring because they can tell you a lot about its general health. Budgies will produce small, flat droppings that appear white in the center with a dark green edge, while larger parrots will produce tubular droppings. These droppings are usually composed of equal amounts of fecal material (the green edge), urine (the clear liquid portion) and urates (the white or cream-colored center). Softbills produce more liquid droppings that are consistent with their fruit-based diets.

Texture and consistency, along with frequency or lack of droppings, can let you know how your pet is feeling. For example, if a parrot eats a lot of fruits and vegetables, its droppings are generally looser and more watery than a bird that eats primarily seeds. But watery droppings can also indicate illness, such as diabetes or kidney problems, that cause a bird to drink more water than usual.

The color of droppings can also give an indication of health. Birds that have psittacosis typically have bright, lime-green droppings, while healthy birds have avocado or darker green and white droppings. Birds with liver problems may produce droppings that are yellowish or reddish, while birds that have internal bleeding will produce dark, tarry droppings. Be aware, however, that a color change doesn't necessarily indicate poor health. For example, parrots that have splurged on a certain fresh food soon have droppings with that food's characteristic color. Birds that overindulge on beets will produce bright red droppings that can look for all the world as though the bird has suffered some serious internal injury. Birds that eat a large quantity of sweet potatoes, blueberries or raspberries produce orange, blue or red droppings, respectively. During pomegranate season, birds that enjoy this fruit develop violet droppings that can look alarming to an unprepared owner.

As part of your daily cage cleaning and observation of your feathered friend, look at its droppings carefully. Learn what is normal for your bird in terms of color, consistency and frequency, and report any changes to your avian veterinarian promptly.

Weekly Tasks

Some of your weekly bird-related chores will include the following:

Removing old food from cage bars and from the corners of the cage where it invariably falls.

Removing, scraping and replacing the perches to keep them clean and free of debris (you might also want to sand them lightly with coarse grain sandpaper to clean them further and improve perch traction for your pet).

Rotating toys in your bird's cage to keep them interesting. Discard any toys that show excessive signs of wear, such as frayed rope, cracked plastic or well-chewed wood.

Cleaning the bird's cage thoroughly. You can simplify the process by placing the cage in the shower and letting hot water from the shower head do some of the work. Be sure to remove your bird, its food and water dishes, its toys and the cage tray paper before putting the cage into the shower. Let the hot water run over the cage for 5 to 10 minutes, then scrub at any stuck-on food with an old toothbrush or some fine-grade steel wool. After you've removed the food and other debris, disinfect the cage with a spray-on disinfectant that you can purchase at your pet store. Make sure to choose a bird-safe product, and read the instructions fully before use.

Rinse the cage thoroughly and dry it completely before returning your bird and its accessories to the cage. (If you have wooden perches in the cage, you can dry them more quickly by placing the wet dowels in a 400°F oven for 10 minutes. Let the perches cool before you put them back in the cage.)

Weather-Related Concerns

Warm weather requires a little extra vigilance on your part to ensure that your pet remains comfortable. To help keep your pet cool, keep it out of direct sun, offer it lots of fresh, juicy vegetables and fruits (be sure to remove these fresh foods from the cage promptly to prevent your bird from eating spoiled food) and mist it lightly with water from a clean spray bottle that is used solely for birdy showers. Offer the showers frequently, and be sure that your pet has adequate time to dry off completely before bedtime.

Warm weather may also bring out a host of insect pests to bedevil you and your bird. Depending on where you live, you may see ants, mosquitoes or other bugs around your bird's cage as the temperature rises. Take care to keep your bird's cage scrupulously clean to discourage any pests, and remove any fresh foods promptly to keep insects out of your bird's food bowl. Finally, in cases of severe infestation, you may have to use Camicide or other bird-safe insecticides to reduce the insect population. (Remove your bird from the area of infestation before spraying.) If the problem becomes severe enough to require professional exterminators, make arrangements to have your bird out of the house for at least 24 hours after spraying has taken place.

You'll also need to pay attention to your bird's needs when the weather turns cooler. You may want to use a heavier cage cover, especially if you lower the heat in your home at bedtime, or you may want to move the bird's cage to another location in your home that is warmer and less drafty.

At least once a year, your bird will lose its feathers. Don't be alarmed because this is a normal process known as molting. Typically, a bird will molt annually, but many pet birds seem to be in a perpetual molt, with feathers falling out and coming in throughout the summer.

You can consider your bird in molting season when you see a lot of whole feathers in the bottom of the cage and you notice that your bird seems to have broken out in a rash of stubbly little aglets (those plastic tips on the ends of your shoelaces). These are the feather sheaths that help new pinfeathers break through the skin, and they are made of keratin (as are our fingernails). The sheaths also help protect growing feathers from damage until the feather completes its growth cycle.

You may notice that your bird is a little more irritable during the molt; this is to be expected. Think about how you would feel if you had all these itchy new feathers coming in all of a sudden. However, your bird may actively seek out more time with you during the molt because owners are handy to have around when a bird has an itch on the top of its head that it can't quite scratch! (Scratch these new feathers gently because some of them may still be growing in and may be sensitive to the touch.) Some birds may benefit from special conditioning foods during the molt; check with your avian veterinarian to see if your bird is a candidate for a special molt diet.

Good Grooming

Your bird has several grooming needs. First, it must be able to bathe regularly. It will also need to have its nails and flight feathers trimmed periodically to ensure its safety.

You can bathe your bird in a variety of ways. You can mist it lightly with warm water, or you can allow it to bathe in the kitchen or bathroom sink under a slow stream of water. Many smaller birds prefer to bathe in their cages, either in a small flat saucer of warm water, a plastic bathtub or an enclosed bird bath that you can purchase in your local pet store. Some birds will roll in damp fresh greens

Bathing is a regular part of your bird's routine in the wild. Some parrots enjoy taking a dip under the bathroom faucet. (PHOTO BY JULIE RACH)

in their food bowls, while others want to jump right in the shower with their owners! Bathing is important to birds to help them keep their feathers clean and healthy, so don't deny your pet the chance to bathe!

Unless your bird has gotten itself into oil, paint, wax or some other substance that elbow grease alone won't remove and that could harm its feathers, it will not require soap as part of its bath. Under routine conditions, soaps and detergents can damage a bird's feathers by removing beneficial oils, so hold the shampoo during your bird's normal cleanup routine!

Let your bird bathe early in the day so it has an opportunity to let its feathers dry completely before bedtime. In cooler weather, you may want help the process along by drying your pet off with a blow dryer to prevent it from becoming chilled after its bath. To do this, set the blow dryer on low and keep it moving so that your bird doesn't become overheated. Your bird may soon learn that drying off is the most enjoyable part of its bath!

Conditioners, anti-picking products and other substances that are applied to your bird's feathers will serve only to encourage your bird to overpreen. Birds do not care to have these products on them and will respond by preening themselves so thoroughly that they might even remove all of their feathers in a particular

---

AVOID MITE PROTECTORS

You may see mite protectors that hang on a bird's cage in pet product catalogs or in your pet store. Well-cared-for pet birds don't have mites and shouldn't be in danger of contracting them. The fumes from some of these products are quite strong and can be harmful to your bird's health. If your pet does have mites, veterinary care is the most effective treatment method.

area. If you want to encourage your bird to preen regularly and help condition its feathers, simply mist the bird regularly with clean, warm water or hold it under a gentle stream from a kitchen or bathroom faucet. Your bird will take care of the rest.

Trimming your bird's nails is a fairly simple procedure. Parrots need their nails clipped occasionally to prevent the nails from catching on toys or perches. Some parrots have light-colored nails, which makes it easier for owners to see where the nail stops and the blood and nerve supply (or quick) begins. In these birds, the quick is generally seen as a pink color inside the nail. If your pet has dark nails, you will need to trim them carefully to keep from cutting them to the quick. An alternative is to file dark nails. You will have to experiment with your pet's likes and dislikes in this area. Some birds don't mind having their nails clipped, but they hate to have them filed. Others are better suited to the file than the clippers, and still others probably wish that their owners would forget the whole nail trimming idea!

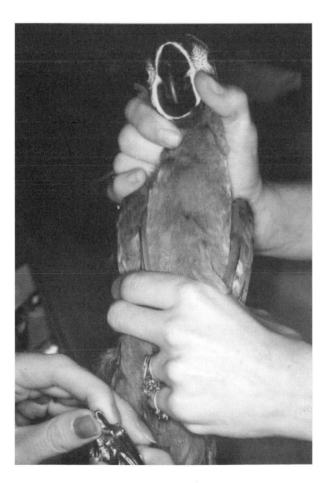

Nail clipping is an important part of parrot grooming. To clip a parrot's nails, you will want to recruit an assistant who knows how to properly restrain the bird. (PHOTO BY GARY A. GALLERSTEIN, DVM)

If your pet is reluctant to have its nails done, you may be able to provide it with a concrete or terra-cotta perch in its cage that will gently file its nails. If you do provide one of these perches for your bird, be sure to watch your bird closely for signs of lameness and remove the abrasive perches if you see your bird's feet are sore or that it seems to be favoring one foot.

You will need to remove only tiny portions of the nail to keep your pet's nails trimmed. Generally, a good guideline to follow is to only remove the hook on each nail, and to do this in the smallest increments possible. Stop well before you reach the quick. If you do happen to cut the nail short enough to make it bleed, apply cornstarch or flour, followed by direct pressure, to stop the bleeding.

The goal of a proper wing trim is to prevent your parrot from flying away or flying into a window, mirror or wall while it's out of its cage. An added benefit of trimming your pet's wings is that its inability to fly well will make it more dependent on you for transportation, which should make it more handleable. However, the bird still needs enough wing feathers so it can glide safely to the ground if it is startled and takes flight from its cage top or play gym.

Wing trims are not usually recommended for finches, softbills and canaries because these pets are usually confined to aviaries, flights or cages. Moreover, the stress of catching these birds for wing trimming generally outweighs the value of the wing trim.

The first time you trim your parrot's wings, you may want to enlist the help of your avian veterinarian to ensure that you do a good job. Wing trimming is a task that must be performed carefully to avoid injuring your pet, so take your time if you're doing it yourself. Please *do not* just take up the largest pair of kitchen shears you own and start snipping away. I have had avian veterinarians tell me about parrots whose owners cut off their birds' wing tips (down to the bone) in this manner.

The first step in wing feather trimming is to assemble all the things you will need and find a quiet, well-lit place to groom your pet before you catch and trim it. Your grooming tools will include:

- a well-worn towel in which to wrap your bird

- small, sharp scissors to do the actual trimming

- needle-nosed pliers (to pull any blood feathers you may cut accidentally)

- flour or cornstarch to act as styptic powder in case a blood feather is cut

- nail trimmers (while you have your bird in the towel, you might as well do its nails, too).

Most parrots also require an assistant trimmer to hold the bird while the trimmer clips the wing feathers.

I encourage you to groom your pet in a quiet, well-lit place because grooming excites some birds and causes them to become wiggly. Good light to work

This macaw is testing its balance following a wing trim. Owners need to monitor the growth of their birds' wing feathers regularly to be aware of when it's time for another trimming. Fully feathered birds are more likely to escape than their clipped counterparts. (PHOTO BY GARY A. GALLERSTEIN, DVM)

under will make your job easier, and a quiet work area may just calm down your pet and make it a bit more handleable.

Once you've assembled your supplies, drape the towel over your hand and catch your parrot with your toweled hand. Grab your bird by the back of its head and neck, and wrap it in the towel. Give it to your assistant and have him hold your bird's head securely with his thumb and index finger. (Having the bird's head covered by the towel will calm it and will give it something to chew on while you clip its wings.)

Lay the bird on its back, being careful not to constrict or compress its chest (remember, birds have no diaphragms to help them breathe), and spread its wing out carefully to look for new feathers that are still growing in, which are also called blood feathers. These can be identified by their waxy, tight look (new feathers in their feather sheaths resemble the end of a shoelace) and their dark centers or quills, which are caused by the blood supply to the new feather.

If your bird has a number of blood feathers, you may want to put off trimming its wings for a few days because older, fully grown feathers act as a cushion to protect those just coming in. If your bird has only one or two blood feathers, you can trim the rest accordingly.

To trim your bird's feathers, separate each one away from the other flight feathers and cut it individually (remember, the goal is to have a well-trimmed bird that's still able to glide a bit if it needs to). Use the primary coverts (the set of feathers above the primary flight feathers on your bird's wing) as a guideline as to how short you can trim.

Cut the first five to eight flight feathers starting from the tip of the wing, and be sure to trim an equal number of feathers from each wing. Chunky birds such as African greys only need to have about five feathers trimmed, while cockatiels and other sleek parrots need to have about eight flight feathers trimmed. Although some people think that a bird needs only one trimmed wing, this is incorrect. A bird that tries to fly with one trimmed and one untrimmed wing may injure itself, and it is far better to trim both wings equally.

Now that you've successfully trimmed your bird's wing feathers, congratulate yourself. You've just taken a great step toward keeping your bird safe. But don't rest on your laurels just yet; you must remember to check your bird's wing feathers monthly and retrim them periodically (about four times a year at a minimum).

IF A BLOOD FEATHER IS CUT

If you do happen to cut a blood feather, remain calm. You must remove it and stop the bleeding to ensure that your bird doesn't bleed to death, and panicking will do neither you nor your bird much good.

To remove a blood feather, take a pair of needle-nosed pliers and grasp the broken feather's shaft as close to the skin of your bird's wing as you can. With one steady motion, pull the feather out completely. After you've removed the feather, put a pinch of flour or cornstarch on the feather follicle (the spot from which you pulled the feather) and apply direct pressure for a few minutes until the bleeding stops. If the bleeding doesn't stop after a few minutes of direct pressure, or if you can't remove the feather shaft, contact your avian veterinarian for further instructions.

Although it may seem like you're hurting your parrot by removing the broken blood feather, consider this: A broken blood feather is like an open faucet. If left in, the faucet stays open and lets the blood out. Once removed, the bird's skin generally closes up behind the feather shaft and shuts off the faucet.

Be particularly alert after a molt because your bird will have a whole new crop of flight feathers that need attention. You'll be able to tell when your pet is due for a trim when it starts becoming bolder in its flying attempts. Right after a wing trim, a parrot generally tries to fly and finds it's unsuccessful at the attempt. It will keep trying, though, and may surprise you one day with a fairly good glide across its cage or off its play gym. If this happens, get the scissors and trim those wings immediately.

Although some people would contend that a bird's beak also needs trimming, I would argue that a healthy bird that has enough chew toys seems to do a remarkable job of keeping its beak trimmed. If, however, your bird's beak becomes overgrown, please consult your avian veterinarian. A parrot's beak contains a surprising number of blood vessels, so beak trimming is best left to the experts. Also, a suddenly overgrown beak may indicate that your bird is suffering from liver damage, a virus or scaly mites, all of which require veterinary care.

What's on the Menu?

The importance of a varied diet cannot be overstressed. Despite some people's long-held ideas, parrots can't prosper on a diet of seeds and water. Think how dull and unhealthy a monotonous diet would be for you—it isn't any more interesting or any healthier for your parrot.

An improper diet causes a number of health problems (respiratory infections, poor feather condition, flaky skin, reproductive problems, to name a few) and is one of the main reasons some parrots live fairly short lives. Some birds fed seed-only diets are prone to undesirable behaviors, such as biting, screaming or chewing. When they are converted to a more balanced diet, these behavior problems decrease and the birds' playfulness and activity levels increase, according to the authors of *Avian Medicine: Principles and Application*.

Here's what the Association of Avian Veterinarians recommends as a healthy parrot diet: 50 percent seed or pellets, grain and legumes; 45 percent dark green or dark orange vegetables and fruits; and 5 percent meat (well cooked, please), eggs (also well cooked) or dairy products. This diet should also serve the needs of finches and canaries well, although finch owners may need to add live food, such as insects, to the menu during breeding season.

The seeds, grain and legumes portion of your parrot's diet can include clean, fresh seed from your local pet supply store. Other items in the bread group that you can offer your pet include unsweetened breakfast cereals, whole-wheat bread, cooked beans, cooked rice and pasta.

Dark green or dark orange vegetables and fruits contain vitamin A, which is an important part of a bird's diet and which is missing from the seeds, grains and legumes group. This vitamin helps fight off infection and keeps a bird's eyes,

Seed-only diets can contribute to behavioral problems, including screaming, feather picking and biting. (PHOTO BY JULIE RACH)

mouth and respiratory system healthy. Some vitamin-A–rich foods are carrots, yams, sweet potatoes, broccoli, dried red peppers, dandelion greens and spinach.

If you've adopted an older bird that eats primarily seeds, try offering your pet some of the fruits and vegetables that are popular with many parrots, such as peeled and seeded apple slices, sliced-open grapes (you can leave grape seeds in) or corn on the cob. Although these fruits and vegetables are not as rich in important vitamins as their dark green or dark orange counterparts, they can help bridge the gap between seeds and a more varied diet for fussy eaters. To ease the stress of relocating to your home, start by feeding your parrot a diet similar to the one it ate in its previous home. Introduce new foods gradually.

You may be wondering whether or not to offer frozen or canned vegetables and fruits to your bird. Some birds will eat frozen vegetables and fruits, while others turn their beaks up at the somewhat mushy texture of these foodstuffs. The high sodium content in some canned foods may make them unhealthy for your

Offering your pet bird a varied diet is a good way to maintain its health, which in turn can have a positive effect on its behavior. (Photo by Julie Rach)

pet. Frozen and canned foods will serve your bird's needs in an emergency, but I would offer only fresh foods on a regular basis.

Along with small portions of the well-cooked meat I mentioned earlier, you can also offer your pet bits of tofu, water-packed tuna, fully scrambled eggs, cottage cheese, unsweetened yogurt or low-fat cheese. Note, however, that a bird's digestive system lacks the enzyme lactase, which results in an inability to fully process dairy foods. Accordingly, it's best to feed dairy products in relatively small quantities.

Whatever healthy fresh foods you offer your parrot, be sure to remove food from the cage promptly to prevent spoilage and to help keep your bird healthy. Ideally, you should change the food in your bird's cage every two to four hours (or as frequently as every 30 minutes in warm weather). Your bird should have a tray of food to pick through in the morning, another to select from during the afternoon and a third fresh salad to nibble on for dinner.

If you don't want to offer your parrot a seed-based diet, perhaps a pelleted food will suit your needs and those of your bird. Pelleted diets are created by mixing a variety of healthful ingredients into a mash and then forcing (or extruding) the hot mixture through a machine to form various shapes. Some pelleted foods have colors and flavors added, while others are fairly plain. These formulated diets provide more balanced nutrition for your pet bird in an easy-to-serve form that reduces the amount of wasted food. They also eliminate the chance for a bird to pick through a smorgasbord of healthy foods to find its favorites and reject the foods of which it isn't particularly fond. Some birds accept pelleted diets quickly, while others require some persuading.

If you want to convert your pet to a pelleted diet, you will want to offer it pellets mixed in with its current diet or as a side dish. (Make sure the bird recognizes that pellets are food before proceeding.) Once you see that your bird is eating the pellets, begin to gradually increase the amount of pellets you offer at mealtime while decreasing the amount of other food you serve. Within a couple of weeks, your bird should be eating its pellets with gusto!

If your parrot seems a bit finicky about trying pellets, you may have to act as if you are enjoying the pellets as a snack in front of your pet. Really play up your apparent enjoyment of this new food because it will pique your pet's curiosity and make the pellets exceedingly interesting.

Whatever you do, don't starve your bird into trying a new food. Offer a variety of new foods consistently, along with familiar favorites. This will ensure that your bird is eating and will also encourage it to try new foods. Don't be discouraged if your parrot doesn't dive right into a new food. Be patient, keep offering new foods to your bird and praise it enthusiastically when it is brave enough to sample something new!

Parrots on pelleted or formulated diets should have all their vitamin and mineral needs met by these special foods, so additional supplements are unnecessary. If your pet's diet is mainly seeds, however, you may want to sprinkle a good-quality vitamin-and-mineral powder onto your pet's fresh foods, where it has the best chance of sticking to the food and being eaten. Vitamin-enriched seed diets may provide some supplementation, but some of these products have the vitamins and minerals added to the seed hull, which your pet will remove and discard while it's eating. Avoid adding vitamin and mineral supplements to your pet's water dish because they can act as a growth medium for bacteria. They may also cause the water to taste different to your bird, which may discourage it from drinking.

Diets for softbills should include a variety of fruits, some vegetables, a good source of protein and plenty of fresh water. Suitable fruit choices include apple, pear, papaya and grapes. Limit the amount of citrus fruits and berries you feed your softbill because the higher acid content of these foods can lead to hemachromatosis or iron storage disease.

Cut up any fruit before serving because your birds will likely swallow the food whole. Chunks of raw dark orange and dark green vegetables can be added to the fruit mixture to provide some variety in your softbill's diet. Protein sources include commercial mynah bird pellets or insects, such as mealworms or crickets.

Some softbills can develop iron storage disease, in which high levels of iron accumulate in the bird's liver. Limit the iron content in your softbill's diet to less than 150 parts per million. Avoid foods with high iron content, such as commercial dog and cat foods, monkey biscuits, raisins and other dried fruits and spinach. Some softbills require nectar as a primary part of their diet, while others enjoy it as an occasional treat.

Visit the Veterinarian Regularly

With good care, a pet parrot may live up to 50 years, although many don't live more than 10 years in captivity. Regular visits to an avian veterinarian will go far to prolong the life of your pet.

As a caring owner, you want your bird to have the best chance at living a long, healthy life. To that end, you will need to locate a veterinarian who understands the special medical needs of birds and with whom you can establish a good working relationship. The best time to do this is when you first purchase your pet. If possible, arrange to visit your veterinarian's office on your way home from the breeder or store. This is particularly important if you have other birds at home, because you don't want to endanger the health of your existing flock or your new pet.

If you don't know an avian veterinarian in your area, ask the person from whom you bought your bird where he takes his birds. Talk to other bird owners you know and find out who they take their pets to, or call bird clubs in your area for referrals.

If you have no bird-owning friends or can't locate a bird club, you might be able to find a veterinarian in the Yellow Pages. Read the advertisements for veterinarians carefully, and try to find one who specializes in birds. Many

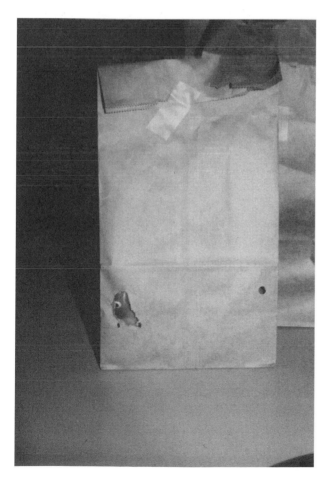

A paper bag is not an appropriate bird carrier—a parrot, such as this Fischer's lovebird, can chew through the bag and escape. Use a proper, safe carrier when taking your pet to visit the veterinarian. (PHOTO BY GARY A. GALLERSTEIN, DVM)

veterinarians who have an interest in treating birds will join the Association of Avian Veterinarians and advertise themselves as members of this organization. Some veterinarians have taken and passed a special examination that entitles them to call themselves avian specialists.

Once you've received your recommendations or found likely candidates in the telephone book, start calling the veterinary offices. Ask the staff how many birds the doctor sees in a week or month, how much an office visit costs and what payment options are available (cash, credit card, check or time payments). You can also inquire if the doctor keeps birds as his or her personal pets.

If you like the answers you receive, make an appointment for your bird to be evaluated. Make a list of any questions you want to ask the doctor regarding diet, how often your bird's wings and nails should be clipped or how often you should bring the bird in for an examination, and take it with you when you go to the appointment.

Be Prepared for Your Visit to the Veterinarian

Bird owners should not be afraid to ask their avian veterinarians questions, but they should also be prepared to provide a good deal of information. When you take your bird in for an exam, the doctor may ask you for answers to these questions:

- Why is the bird here today?
- How would you describe the bird's normal activity level?
- How is the bird's appetite?
- What does the bird's normal diet consist of?
- Have you noticed a change in the bird's appearance lately?

Be sure to explain any changes in as much detail as you can because changes in your bird's typical behavior can indicate illness.

During the initial examination, the veterinarian will probably take his or her first look at your pet bird while it is still in its cage or carrier. The doctor may talk to you and your bird for a few minutes to give the bird an opportunity to become accustomed to him or her, rather than simply reaching right in and grabbing your pet. While the veterinarian is talking to you, he or she will check the bird's posture and its ability to perch.

Next, the doctor should remove the bird from its carrier or cage and look it over carefully. He or she will particularly note the condition of your pet's eyes, its beak and its nares (nostrils). The bird should be weighed, and the veterinarian will probably palpate (feel) your pet's body and wings for any lumps, bumps or deformities that require further investigation. Feather condition will also be assessed, as will the condition of the bird's vent, legs and feet. Your veterinarian will also listen to your pet's lungs with a stethoscope, and he or she may also check the bird's mouth, throat and ears.

After your veterinarian has completed your bird's physical examination, he or she may recommend further tests. These can include:

- Blood tests, which help a doctor determine if your bird has a specific disease. From a blood test, the doctor can obtain a complete blood count, showing the number of red and white blood cells that your bird has. This information can help diagnose infections or anemia.

- Radiographs or x-rays, which allow a veterinarian to study the size and shape of a bird's internal organs, along with the formation of its bones. X-rays also help doctors find foreign bodies in a bird's system.

- Microbiological exams, which help a veterinarian determine if any unusual organisms (bacteria, fungi or yeast) are growing inside your bird's body.

- Fecal analysis, which evaluates a small sample of your bird's droppings to determine if it has internal parasites or a bacterial or yeast infection.

Once the examination is concluded and you've had a chance to discuss any questions you have with your veterinarian, the doctor will probably recommend a follow-up examination schedule for your pet. Most healthy birds visit the veterinarian annually, but your doctor may recommend a different schedule.

To keep your pet from suffering long-term health risks, keep a close eye on its daily activities and appearance. If something suddenly changes in the way your bird looks or acts, contact your veterinarian immediately.

Bird First Aid

It is always a good idea to be prepared for an emergency situation. With quick thinking and even quicker action, you may be able to help save your bird from serious injury or death.

No matter what the situation, there are a few fundamentals to remember when facing a medical emergency with your pet. First, keep as calm as possible. Your bird is already excited enough from being injured, and an agitated response from you will not help your pet get well. Next, stop any bleeding, keep the bird warm and try not to handle the bird more than is necessary.

After you've stopped any bleeding and made sure your bird is warm, call your veterinarian's office for further instructions. Describe what happened to your pet as clearly and calmly as you can. Listen carefully to the instructions you are given and follow them. Finally, transport your bird to the veterinarian's office as quickly and safely as you can.

A BIRD FIRST-AID KIT

- appropriate-sized towels for catching and holding your bird

- a heating pad, heat lamp or other heat source

- a pad of paper and pencil to make notes about the bird's condition

- styptic powder, silver nitrate stick, flour or cornstarch to stop bleeding (use styptic powder and silver nitrate stick on beak and nails only)

- blunt-tipped scissors

- nail clippers and nail file

- needle-nosed pliers to pull broken blood feathers

- blunt-end tweezers

- hydrogen peroxide or other disinfectant solution

- eye irrigation solution

- bandage materials such as gauze squares, masking tape (it doesn't stick to a bird's feathers like adhesive tape does) and gauze rolls

- Pedialyte or other energy supplement

- eye dropper

- syringes to irrigate wounds or feed sick birds

Keep all these supplies in one place, such as a fishing tackle box. This will eliminate your having to search for some supplies in emergency situations, and the case can be taken along to bird shows, on trips or left for the bird-sitter if your bird isn't a traveler.

Here are some urgent medical situations that bird owners are likely to encounter, the reason that they are medical emergencies, the signs and symptoms your bird might show and the recommended treatments for the problem:

Animal Bite

If your bird is bitten, infections can develop from bacteria on the biting animal's teeth and/or claws. Also, a bird's internal organs can be damaged by the bite.

SIGNS THAT INDICATE A PROBLEM

Often there are no signs of injury, but on occasion you will be able to actually see the bite marks.

STEPS TO TAKE

Call your veterinarian's office and transport the bird there immediately. Treatment for shock and antibiotics are often the course of action veterinarians take to save birds that have been bitten.

Beak Injury

A bird needs both its upper and lower beak (also called the upper and lower mandible) to eat and preen properly. Infections can also set in rather quickly if a beak is fractured or punctured.

SIGNS THAT INDICATE A PROBLEM

Bird is bleeding from its beak. This often occurs after the bird flies into a windowpane or mirror, or if it has a run-in with an operational ceiling fan. Bird may

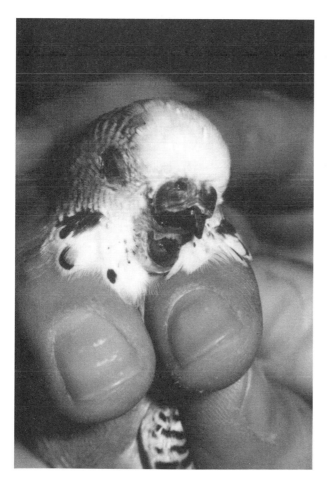

This unfortunate budgie lost its beak to the wrath of a larger bird. Be careful when allowing birds, particularly those of different species, to interact. (PHOTO BY GARY A. GALLERSTEIN, DVM)

also have a cracked or otherwise damaged beak, and portions of the beak may be missing.

STEPS TO TAKE

Control the bleeding. Keep the bird calm and quiet. Contact your avian veterinarian's office.

Bleeding

Uncontrolled bleeding can become a life-threatening situation.

SIGNS THAT INDICATE A PROBLEM

In the event of external bleeding, you will see blood on the bird, its cage and its surroundings. In the case of internal bleeding, the bird may pass bloody droppings or bleed from its nose, mouth or vent.

STEPS TO TAKE

For external bleeding, apply direct pressure. If the bleeding doesn't stop with direct pressure, apply a coagulant, such as styptic powder (for nails and beaks) or cornstarch (for broken feathers and skin injuries). If the bleeding stops, observe the bird to make sure that it does not start bleeding again and for signs of shock. Call your veterinarian's office if the bird seems weak or if it has lost a lot of blood and arrange to take the bird in for further treatment.

In the case of broken blood feathers, you may have to remove the feather shaft to stop the bleeding. To do this, grasp the feather shaft as close to the skin as you can with a pair of needle-nosed pliers and pull out the shaft with a swift, steady motion. Apply a bit of flour or cornstarch to stop the bleeding, and then apply direct pressure to the skin.

Breathing Difficulty

Respiratory problems in pet birds can be life-threatening.

SIGNS THAT INDICATE A PROBLEM

The bird wheezes or clicks while breathing, bobs its tail, breathes with an open mouth, has a discharge from its nares or swelling around its eyes.

STEPS TO TAKE

Keep the bird warm, place it in a bathroom with a hot shower running to help it breathe easier and call your veterinarian's office.

Burns

A sufficiently sever burn can cause your bird to go into shock and die.

SIGNS THAT INDICATE A PROBLEM

A burned bird has reddened skin and burnt or greasy feathers. The bird may also show signs of shock (see below for details).

STEPS TO TAKE

Mist the burned area with cool water. Lightly apply an antibiotic cream or spray. Do not apply any oily or greasy substances, including butter. If the bird seems shocky or the burn is widespread, contact your veterinarian's office for further instructions.

Concussion

A concussion results from a sharp blow to the head that can cause injury to the brain.

SIGNS THAT INDICATE A PROBLEM

Birds sometimes suffer concussions when they fly into mirrors or windows. They will seem stunned and may go into shock.

STEPS TO TAKE

Keep the bird warm, prevent it from hurting itself further and watch it carefully. Alert your veterinarian's office to the injury.

Cloacal Prolapse

When a cloacal prolapse occurs, you will see the bird's lower intestines, uterus or cloaca protruding from its vent.

SIGNS THAT INDICATE A PROBLEM

The bird has pink, red, brown or black tissue protruding from its vent.

STEPS TO TAKE

Contact your veterinarian's office for immediate care. Your veterinarian can usually reposition the organs.

Egg Binding

When an egg becomes bound, the egg blocks the hen's excretory system and makes it impossible for her to eliminate. Moreover, eggs can break inside the hen, which can lead to infection.

SIGNS THAT INDICATE A PROBLEM

An egg-bound hen strains to lay eggs unsuccessfully. She becomes fluffed and lethargic, sits on the floor of her cage, may be paralyzed and may have a swollen abdomen.

Steps to Take

Keep the hen warm because this may help her pass the egg. Put her and her cage into a warm bathroom with a hot shower running to increase the humidity, which may also help alleviate the problem. If your bird doesn't improve shortly (within an hour), contact your veterinarian.

Eye Injury

An untreated eye problem may lead to blindness.

Signs that Indicate a Problem

Swollen or pasty eyelids, discharge, cloudy eyeball, increased rubbing of eye area.

Steps to Take

Examine the eye carefully for foreign bodies. Contact your veterinarian for more information.

Fractures

In addition to the obvious problems attendant to a broken bone, a fracture can cause a bird to go into shock. Depending on the type of fracture, infections can also set in.

Signs that Indicate a Problem

Birds most often break bones in their legs, so be on the lookout for a bird that is holding one leg at an odd angle or that isn't putting weight on one leg. Sudden swelling of a leg or wing or a droopy wing can also indicate fractures.

Steps to Take

Confine the bird to its cage or a small carrier. Don't handle it unnecessarily. Keep it warm and contact your veterinarian.

Frostbite

A bird can lose toes or feet to frostbite. It can also go into shock and die as a result.

Signs that Indicate a Problem

The frostbitten area is very cold and dry to the touch and is pale in color.

Steps to Take

Warm the damaged tissue up gradually in a circulating water bath. Keep the bird warm and contact your veterinarian's office for further instructions.

Ingested Foreign Object

SIGNS THAT INDICATE A PROBLEM
You may not notice anything wrong with your bird, but if you notice that you cannot locate a small toy or other item with which the bird was playing, it may have mistakenly eaten the object.

STEPS TO TAKE
Immediately contact your veterinarian's office.

Inhaled Foreign Object
Birds can develop serious respiratory problems from foreign objects in their bodies.

SIGNS THAT INDICATE A PROBLEM
Wheezing and/or other difficulty breathing.

STEPS TO TAKE
If you suspect that your bird has inhaled something it shouldn't, contact your veterinarian's office immediately.

Lead Poisoning
Lead poisoning can be lethal to birds.

SIGNS THAT INDICATE A PROBLEM
A bird with lead poisoning may act depressed or weak. It may become blind, or it may walk in circles at the bottom of its cage. It may regurgitate or pass droppings that resemble tomato juice.

STEPS TO TAKE
Contact your avian veterinarian immediately. Treatment for lead poisoning must begin shortly after exposure for the bird's best chance of survival. It may require several days or weeks to complete successfully.

Note: Lead poisoning is easily prevented by keeping birds away from common sources of lead in the home. These include stained-glass items, leaded paint found in some older homes, fishing weights, drapery weights and some parrot toys (some are weighted with lead)! Note that "lead" pencils will not cause lead poisoning (they're actually graphite).

Overheating
An overly high body temperature can be lethal to a bird.

Signs that Indicate a Problem

An overheated bird will hold its wings away from its body, open its mouth and roll its tongue in an attempt to cool itself. Birds don't have sweat glands, so they must try to cool their bodies by exposing as much of their skin's surface as they can to moving air.

Steps to Take

Cool the bird off by putting it in front of a fan (make sure the blades are screened so the bird doesn't injure itself further), by spraying it with cool water or by having it stand in a bowl of cool water. Let the bird drink cool water if it can (if it can't, offer it cool water with an eyedropper) and contact your veterinarian.

Poisoning

Obviously, any animal that consumes a poisonous substance is in danger. A poisoned bird can die quickly.

Signs that Indicate a Problem

Poisoned birds may suddenly regurgitate, have diarrhea or bloody droppings and have redness or burns around their mouths. They may also go into convulsions, become paralyzed or go into shock.

Steps to Take

Put the poison out of your bird's reach. Contact your veterinarian for further instructions. Be prepared to take the poison with you to the doctor's office in case he or she needs to contact a poison control center for further information.

Seizures

Seizures can indicate a number of serious conditions, including lead poisoning, infection, nutritional deficiency, heat stroke and epilepsy.

Signs that Indicate a Problem

The bird goes into a seizure that lasts from a few seconds to a minute. Afterward, it seems dazed and may stay on the cage floor for several hours. It may also appear unsteady and unable to perch.

Steps to Take

Keep the bird from hurting itself further by removing everything you can from its cage. Cover the bird's cage with a towel and darken the room to reduce the bird's stress level. Contact your veterinarian's office for further instructions immediately.

Shock

Shock indicates that the bird's circulatory system cannot move the blood supply around the bird's body. This is a serious condition that can lead to death if left untreated.

Signs that Indicate a Problem

Shocky birds may act depressed, may breathe rapidly and may have a fluffed appearance. If your bird displays one or more of these signs in conjunction with a recent accident, suspect shock and take appropriate action.

Steps to Take

Keep your bird warm, cover its cage and transport it to your veterinarian's office as soon as possible.

In *The Complete Bird Owner's Handbook,* veterinarian Gary Gallerstein offers the following advice to bird owners whose birds need urgent care:

DON'T GIVE A BIRD HUMAN MEDICATIONS OR MEDICATIONS PRESCRIBED FOR ANOTHER ANIMAL UNLESS SO DIRECTED BY YOUR VETERINARIAN.

DON'T GIVE YOUR BIRD MEDICATIONS THAT ARE SUGGESTED BY A FRIEND, A STORE EMPLOYEE OR A HUMAN PHYSICIAN.

DON'T GIVE A BIRD ALCOHOL OR LAXATIVES.

DON'T APPLY ANY OILS OR OINTMENTS TO YOUR BIRD UNLESS YOUR VETERINARIAN TELLS YOU TO DO SO.

DON'T BATHE A SICK BIRD.

Bird Showing

You've really come to enjoy your pet bird and other bird owners you've met through visits to your favorite bird supply store and your avian veterinarian's office. You want to take the next step—showing your bird—but you're unsure of how to go about it.

Most of the birds shown in competition are canaries, finches and softbills and the smaller parrots, such as budgies and cockatiels.

The first step a novice bird exhibitor should take is to join a bird club. Attend meetings of your local bird club to meet exhibitors who are willing to help people new to showing birds (like you). Go to bird shows as an observer and watch the judging. Talk to the breeders of winning birds after the show to see if they have chicks available that you can purchase. Ask the breeder of your birds, as well as other breeders in the club, to help you start training your birds for the show season. Bird showing is most active in the fall.

Once you have obtained some promising show birds, locate shows through bird magazines, club newsletters and even bulletin boards in pet stores and veterinary offices. Announcements will usually include a contact person's name, address and phone number along with the date and location of the event. Call or write this person to obtain a show catalog, which is your guide to the particulars of the show you've chosen to enter.

The show catalog will contain the judging standard for the birds that will be shown. The standard describes an ideal of perfection for each type of bird being shown. So far, this ideal bird does not yet exist, but breeders keep trying.

Once you have an idea of the qualities that the judges are looking for, how do you get your bird to live up to its own standard of perfection? You train it and groom it and show it off in a proper show cage.

Show birds must demonstrate grace under pressure during judging. They must appear calm, but alert, and comfortable in their show cages (which may or may not be their regular cages). They must also be able to accept and adjust to a stranger looking closely at them and tapping on their cages. Finally, they must be in perfect feather and tip-top overall condition. Sounds like a tall order? It is, but it can be done!

To train your bird for the show circuit, get it accustomed to its show cage well before show season starts. Several months before its first show, put your pet's show cage where your bird can see it. Gradually move the show cage closer to your bird's home. When your bird appears curious about, but not afraid of, the show cage, put it in the show cage with the cage door open. Allow your pet to explore the new cage, but encourage it to stay on its perch.

After your bird has learned to stay on the perch, invite some friends over to simulate a show. Reinforce your pet's good behavior (staying on its perch and not showing signs of panic) with praise and a small treat after "the show."

Next, ask a friend to "judge" your bird. Have this person get close to the cage and give your bird a thorough visual inspection. Ask the "judge" to tap lightly on the show cage with a pointer or pencil and to poke gently at the bird with this object. Praise your bird for its good behavior. (If, however, your bird seems uncomfortable with this added attention, you may want to reconsider the show circuit for this bird.)

After you have your bird trained, you'll need to work on its grooming. To show successfully, it will need to be fully feathered, have its wings and nails

---

PARROTS AND ALLERGIES

Cockatoos, African greys and cockatiels are among the "dustier" parrots and should probably be avoided if a family member has allergies. In the course of daily grooming and preening, parrots can raise a small cloud of dust and dander that may be irritating to some allergy sufferers' sinuses and respiratory systems.

Children and birds can get along nicely if the initial introductions are properly handled. (PHOTO BY PAMELA L. HIGDON)

trimmed and its feet clean. Its eyes will need to be bright and clear, and its nares will need to be free of dust and debris. If your bird suddenly breaks out in pin-feathers, you may want to reconsider showing it at that time, or you may want to still enter the show as practice.

Parrots and Children

Children and parrots may be a natural mix, or they may lead each other into temptation. Children's sudden movements, outbursts of energy and loud voices may excite a boisterous cockatoo or macaw into joining into the fun. On the other hand, quieter parrots may suffer stress by being around children and may start to demonstrate problem behaviors, such as feather picking or screaming.

Children may be startled by a parrot's loud squawks. It is not at all unlikely that they will be unintentionally injured when they poke their fingers into a bird's cage because the bird may bite them to defend its territory. Explain to the child that the cage is the bird's home and that it doesn't like being annoyed by being poked at. Tell the child that bird bites hurt and that a bird's beak is capable of doing damage, particularly if the beak belongs to a cockatoo or macaw. Other birds have a tendency to pinch when they bite, which means the bite hurts, but it doesn't cause a particularly serious injury.

Children and parrots can interact well under the right conditions. Friends of mine who have a 3-year-old grandson have made sure that the boy knows which birds in their flock are child-friendly and which ones bite. One of the veterinarians who used to care for my bird would let his children hold her, but only if they sat very still and held her carefully on their laps. Because her previous interactions with children were not this well supervised, I was impressed with her progress regarding children and pleased with their ability to handle her so gently and carefully.

Veterinarian, bird owner and parent Gary Gallerstein suggests that intelligence and guidance are the keys to allowing children and birds to interact safely. Remind your children that birds are intelligent creatures worthy of respect and that birds should never be teased or poked. Above all, adults must try to prevent problems before they occur and be ready to intervene to keep both children and birds safe from each other.

Some simple rules for children to follow will greatly enhance the child/bird relationship. Parents should make sure children know to:

1. Approach the cage quietly. Birds don't like to be surprised.

2. Talk softly to the bird. Don't scream or yell at it.

3. Avoid shaking or hitting the cage.

4. Avoid poking at the bird or its cage with fingers, sticks, pencils or other items.

5. Handle the bird gently if the child is allowed to take the bird out of its cage.

6. Keep the bird inside. In unfamiliar surroundings (such as the outdoors), birds can become confused and fly away from their owners. Most are never recovered.

7. Respect the bird's need for quiet time.

In *My Parrot, My Friend,* Bonnie Munro Doane and Thomas Qualkinbush offer the following guidelines about parrots and children:

1. The parrot should be the sole responsibility of the adult who acquired it. It is unfair to expect a child to provide the care these birds require without ongoing supervision in the adult's presence.

2. Never leave a child alone with any parrot, regardless of how tame the bird is.

3. If you wish to allow your child to pet the parrot, the bird should be perched on the adult's arm, and the adult should have full control of the bird's head.

4. Young hand-reared parrots may be allowed to perch on a child's arm, but only after the adult has made a decision about safety for both child and bird.

5. Practice good hygiene in handling birds and children. Do not touch your child after cleaning the cage unless you have first washed your hands. Conversely, do not handle the parrot after changing an infant's diapers without first washing your hands.

A PET IS *NOT* A GOOD GIFT

Please do not give any live pet as a present. Birthdays, Christmas, Hanukkah and other holidays are exciting, but stressful, times for both people and animals.

A pet coming to a new home is under enough stress just by joining its new family; don't add to its stress by bringing it home for a holiday. Instead, give the child pet care accessories for the actual celebration and a gift certificate that will allow the child to select his or her pet (with proper parental permission and supervision, of course) after the excitement of the special day has tempered.

Other Pets and Parrots

In addition to people in the home, a parrot may be exposed to other pets. Practicing some basic safety guidelines will help to keep peace in your animal kingdom.

Supervise all interactions between pets. Do not allow your bird to be out on the floor of your home unattended (not only does this protect your bird from other pets, but it also keeps it from being stepped on by humans or from injuring itself).

Cats may be attracted to the quick movements of smaller birds, such as canaries, budgies or cockatiels. We've all seen Sylvester in the Warner Brothers cartoons try to catch Tweety Pie, and I can attest to the fact that cats like to watch budgies from watching my own childhood pets. Fluff, our Manx cat, thought budgie watching was great fun, and he even managed to knock over my budgie Charlie's cage and stand. Larger parrots, such as Amazons, macaws or cockatoos, may be less threatened by cats, but I would not recommend leaving any bird alone with a cat. Although clipped wings are generally regarded as a safety precaution for birds, in the case of interactions with cats, clipped wings can be a decided disadvantage. For the safety of all pets, closely watch your cat when it's around your birds. Regardless of your bird's size, a curious cat could claw or bite your pet.

Many experts believe that a dog and a parrot can be taught to coexist peacefully, especially if the bird is one of the larger parrots. You may even find the relationship beneficial if your dog helps you clean up the vegetables your bird throws out of its food bowl and onto the floor in the course of a day. Keep in mind, though, that some sight hounds and other hunting breeds may want to hunt or chase your bird as part of an instinctive behavior.

I know of an Ibizan Hound that could only visit my veterinarian on "bird-free" days. Before the dog arrived, the office mascot (an Amazon parrot) had to be caged—the dog had quite strong hunting instincts. Yet, a Greyhound I know has lived peacefully with a ringnecked parrot and a kakariki for many years. She has never shown any desire to hunt these birds.

Owners should supervise interactions between dogs and parrots at all times because a dog could step on the bird accidentally or bite it. Make sure to keep an eye on your dog around your bird's cage, too, so that your enthusiastic canine pet doesn't send bird, cage and stand flying as it gallops through the living room. In many cases, parrots will learn how to take control of a relationship with a dog, and your bird may take special joy in calling for your dog as you do or imitating your dog's barking.

Other types of pets, such as small exotic mammals and reptiles, are rather new companion animals, and there is little reliable information about how these animals fare with birds. Some bird experts believe that ferrets do not make good bird companions because the ferrets have a highly developed hunting instinct that they cannot overcome. Most reptiles should leave pet birds alone, but any interactions between pet birds and medium- to large-size snakes should be monitored carefully.

Finally, if your bird tangles with another pet in your home, contact your avian veterinarian immediately. Emergency treatment (for bacterial infection from a puncture wound or shock from being stepped on or suffering a broken bone) may be required to save your feathered friend's life.

Tips for a Well-Behaved Bird

Don't encourage your bird to misbehave. Take some time to analyze your bird's setup and how you interact with it to ensure that you haven't unwittingly created some potential behavior problems.

First, check the height of the cage. Is it high enough so the bird feels secure, but not so high that you can't easily reach the bird? Does the bird have a height advantage over you and other members of your family? Remember, birds behave for those they look up to and mistreat those they look down upon.

If you have a high cage and your family is vertically challenged, you may have to raise the height of your family by building a step for shorter people to stand on. This will equalize their height with the bird's and also equalize their status in the flock with that of your bird.

Next, do you swoop down on your bird from above? Swooping your hands down on your bird without warning imitates the action of a predatory bird in the wild, which can cause a bird to try to defend itself. Also, many species feel threatened if they are picked up in such a way that their wings are constricted or held against their bodies. Be sure to warn your bird that you are in the area, and allow it to step on your hand by using the "up" and "down" commands, rather than just whisking it out of its cage or off its play gym at your whim.

Another problem behavior owners demonstrate toward their birds is to poke or gesture at them. Finger-pointing and extensive gesturing is threatening to people—your bird feels the same way and will react by trying to defend itself from you. It interprets fingers being poked in its face as an invitation to fight and will do so by striking at or biting the offending fingers.

Many bird owners unintentionally antagonize their birds with big gestures, then they act surprised when their pets bite them. Consider your body language when you're spending time around your bird. Some birds react badly to acrylic fingernails or brightly colored polish, while others will try to preen their owners' nails. If your bird suddenly starts acting strangely about your hands, you may have to get rid of your artificial nails or change the color of your polish. Discourage your pet from preening polished nails because it can possibly poison itself by ingesting some of the polish.

Owners who do not respect their birds' need for privacy and quiet can create a variety of bad bird behaviors. If you want to stay up and watch television after your bird has been put to bed, you may have to move into another room to give your bird a chance to settle down and sleep. If you don't give your bird an opportunity to have time to itself and to get adequate amounts of sleep, don't be surprised if it starts to scream or bite. It may simply be trying to tell you it needs a dark, quiet time in which to rest and sleep in order to maintain its health and good humor.

While we're on the subject of rest, be sure to let your bird have adequate periods of rest throughout the day as well as at night. Remember that if your bird doesn't get all the rest it needs, it may be irritable and it may be more prone to misbehaving when it's tired. Also consider your bird's feelings during times of stress, such as breeding or molting. Your bird's body is going through changes during these periods, and it may become somewhat nippier during them.

If your parrot misbehaves and you laugh at it, you may be rewarding the misbehavior without meaning to. The important thing to do when your bird misbehaves (no matter how cute the misbehavior is the first time you see it) is to provide appropriate discipline for your pet to discourage it from behaving badly. To do this, look sternly at your pet and say "Stop it!" in a firm tone or put the bird in "time-out" for a few minutes. You have to determine which form of discipline will work the best with your parrot.

Owners may also unintentionally reinforce bad behavior in their pets in other ways. If a young bird reaches out with its beak to test the perching potential of its owner's arm (remember that young birds like to taste or test things with their beaks) and the owner pulls away, the bird will soon learn that its beak has the

HOW TO DISCIPLINE YOUR PARROT

- Cover its cage for no more than 10 minutes to quiet it down

- Look sternly at it and tell it "No"

- Reward it—lots of verbal praise, petting or occasional food treats—when it behaves in a way that pleases you

- Put it in its cage and ignore it for no more than 10 minutes

- Rotate your wrist gently to put the bird slightly off balance if it bites you while it's on your hand

- Be consistent in your disciplinary measures

power to intimidate people, and it will use that power for its own ends. By pulling away, the owner may also be telling the bird that owners can't be trusted when they put out their hands for the bird to step up on.

Don't allow your pet to become overly bonded to a single person or a single area in your home. Cagebound parrots will defend their homes viciously, and people who are perceived as the parrot's mate will suffer greatly during the parrot's breeding season. All members of the family should take part in caring for the bird to discourage it from bonding too closely with any one member of the family, and the bird should have a variety of locations in the home that it can consider its own—its cage in one room, its play gym in another and perhaps a portable perch on wheels that can move from room to room—in order to keep it from perceiving any one place in the home as its territory that requires defending.

Make sure you are clear and consistent with your discipline, or your bird will be confused and may be tempted to misbehave so it can see what kind of response you will give it. When you want the bird to step up onto your hand, for example, simply say, "Up," or, "Step up." Don't sputter and putter out a string of "ups" that sound like a misfiring motor. Birds understand simple, clear direction.

Don't overdiscipline your pet. For example, if you put your bird in time-out because it was screaming, make sure to uncover the cage within 10 minutes of covering it, or the discipline will be ineffective. Your parrot needs quick, effective correction when it misbehaves. A brief denial of your attention and affection is often quite effective. A few minutes under a cage cover or a stern look from a beloved owner go a long way toward modifying your pet's behavior.

Finally, how many birds do you have in your home? How many do you want? How many do you really have time for? Granted, parrots are attractive, interesting pets, and many people want several of them in their homes. I'd love to have

HOW *NOT* TO DISCIPLINE
YOUR PARROT

- Yell at it

- Hit it

- Lock it in a dark room for hours

- Throw it on the ground

- Throw its cage around

- Throw things at its cage

- Spray water on it

- Handle it roughly

- Send mixed messages of discipline

more than the one bird that I presently own, but I learned early on that I have a one-bird limit. My parrot requires a great deal of time and attention from me, and it wouldn't be fair to either her or to me to try to add more birds to our household because the relationship I have with my bird would suffer greatly.

Remember that each parrot is an individual that requires a certain amount of time and attention from its owner each day, and you may be unintentionally setting yourself up to be a disappointed owner if you end up with a flock of parrots that misbehave because they are all vying for your attention. Keep in mind, too, that more parrots means more parrot food, parrot cages, parrot toys and avian vet bills, all of which can drain your resources considerably.

Most of all, appreciate your pet bird for the wonderful creature that it is. Don't become overly stressed when your bird acts like a bird, even if that means that it bites or screams from time to time. If you become stressed about these infrequent episodes, your bird will sense it and you will be creating a vicious cycle that neither of you will enjoy and which will be difficult to modify.

Both you and your bird will enjoy your relationship far more when you accept that neither of you is perfect, but you are both terrific individuals that make an even better pair!

PET BIRD PERSONALITIES

African Greys

As their name suggests, African greys come from Africa and are predominantly gray birds with red tails. These highly intelligent parrots are regarded throughout the bird keeping world for their talking abilities, although no bird is guaranteed to talk.

On the negative side, greys are prone to feather picking and produce powder down, which can cause allergic reactions in some people.

Greys may become bonded to one person in the home. They are also prone to becoming stressed if they sense tension in the home or if a routine is not established for them. Greys can be high-strung, and they are often suspicious of new people, although they become accustomed to strangers rather quickly.

Greys need good-sized cages, plenty of toys and ample time out of their cages with their owners. Their diet should consist of a good-quality seed mix or pellets, supplemented with a variety of fresh foods. Greys may need more calcium in their diets than other parrots. You can provide your grey with calcium by sprinkling a supplement on its fresh foods, by offering it a cuttlebone in its cage or by adding calcium-rich foods, such as broccoli, almonds, soybeans, tofu and collard greens, to your grey's diet.

Amazons

Amazons are medium-sized, chunky green parrots from Latin America. They are noted for their talking and singing skills and can be quite outgoing birds, singing opera or performing tricks for people outside of the family flock.

Amazons are playful birds that enjoy human companionship, and they will tolerate cuddling on their terms.

Amazons may be aggressive during breeding season. They can also bond to a single person in the home. They can be strong willed and stubborn and enjoy being the dominant creature in the parrot-owner relationship.

Amazon owners need to watch the amount of fat their birds consume because Amazons are natural snackers and can become obese. A pelleted diet supplemented with a variety of fresh fruits and vegetables should help keep an Amazon in shape. These parrots need roomy cages with interesting toys and time out of their cages on play gyms or with their owners to keep mentally and physically fit.

Brotogeris

The *Brotogeris* (pronounced bro-toe-JER-us) genus, which includes grey-cheeked, bee bee and canary-winged parakeets, are small green birds from Mexico and South America. This genus has also been described as "pocket parrots" because of their small sizes and their fondness for hiding in the pockets of their owners' shirts.

Brotogeris make bold pets. They can become very attached to their owners, and they can learn to be noisy if this behavior is reinforced. *Brotogeris* like to climb, and they are strong fliers, so be sure to keep a pet *Brotogeris*'s wings clipped.

Some grey cheeks can be nippy if they are not handled regularly. Grey cheeks frequently bathe in their water bowls and can bathe themselves right out of drinking water. Their diet should include a good-quality seed mix or pellets, supplemented with fresh foods. They need medium-sized cages and ample time out of their cages to interact and play with their owners.

Budgerigars

The budgerigar, commonly called a parakeet, hails from Australia. It has been kept in captivity since the 1840s and has been raised in captivity for more than 100 years because Australia stopped exporting their perky little parrots in the 1890s. The budgie is the most commonly kept pet bird in the world.

Budgies are noted for their talking ability, but owners may have to listen carefully to hear their birds' small voices. Budgies can be kept singly, in pairs or in community aviaries. They are good pets for novice bird owners because of their small sizes and their relatively uncomplicated care regimens.

Despite their small sizes, budgies need a good-sized cage in order to exercise properly, or they need out-of-cage time every day during which they can play and interact with their owners.

A balanced budgie diet includes seeds or pellets supplemented with an assortment of fresh fruits and vegetables. Budgies are particularly fond of millet sprays as a treat!

Caiques

Caiques (pronounced ky-EEKs) are small, highly active parrots from South America. These intelligent little parrots have good appetites and a tendency to taste almost anything and everything around them. Noted chewers, caiques need to have plenty of toys to destroy. They are also known to be strong willed and may get out of control quickly without having guidelines set by their owners. They are not shy about making themselves heard when the situation presents itself.

Caiques need good-sized cages and time to interact regularly with their owners outside of the cage. Their diets should include fresh foods, along with a good-quality seed mix or pellets.

Canaries

Canaries are small cage birds that originally came from the Canary Islands off Africa. They have been kept in captivity since the 1400s and are thoroughly domesticated.

Canaries have been kept in captivity since the 1400s.
(PHOTO BY ERIC ILASENKO)

Breeders concentrate on different attributes in their canary lines. Some breed canaries for shape and stance, while others breed canaries for their colorful feathers (along with the familiar yellow, canaries are also available with white, red, orange or brownish feathers). Still others breed song canaries for their lovely singing abilities.

If you want a singing canary, you will have to locate a male bird. Make arrangements with the breeder or store to return the bird if it proves to be a nonsinger. Keep in mind that males sing to attract females. If canaries are kept in pairs, males won't sing.

Cockatiels

Second only in popularity to budgies, cockatiels are also from Australia. These slender, crested parrots are known for their whistling ability and their gentle natures. The cockatiel's small size and fairly quiet voice make it a good option for apartment dwellers who want a pet bird.

Cockatiels like to interact with their owners, but on the bird's terms, not the human's. They are good candidates for community aviaries and may be ideal choices for people seeking their first birds.

Cockatiels can be prone to night frights or thrashing episodes and feather picking. They also produce powder down, which can cause allergic reactions in some people.

Cockatiels need a varied diet that includes a good-quality seed mixture or pellets, along with fresh fruits and vegetables. Some cockatiels are notorious for being seed-only eaters, so start your young birds off right! A cockatiel's cage should be roomy enough to allow the bird to exercise, or you should make arrangements for your pet to have regular out-of-cage play sessions because these active little parrots need their exercise.

Cockatoos

Cockatoos originated in Australia. These crested white or pink birds are sure to attract attention with their striking appearance and cuddly personalities.

Be warned that these feathered teddy bears are not necessarily the "loves" they appear to be. Male cockatoos can kill mates during breeding season. They can demonstrate sexual frustration with people during breeding season, biting the person in the home they perceive as their "mate." Cockatoos are also prone to screaming, feather picking and self-mutilation. Moluccans may experience night frights or thrashing episodes.

Cockatoos require a great deal of attention from, interaction with and guidance from their owners or they are likely to become downright unmanageable. First-time bird owners may be surprised, or even disappointed, in the amount of attention cockatoos demand. Cockatoos produce powder down, which can cause allergic reactions in some people.

Cockatoos need large, secure cages. These intelligent parrots are natural escape artists, so you may have to provide additional locks on your bird's cage besides the latch on its door. Cockatoo diets should include good-quality seeds or pellets supplemented with fresh fruits and vegetables.

Conures

Conures are small parrots from South America. They are available in a variety of colors, ranging from muted greens to brilliant oranges. They are inquisitive little birds that offer something for almost anyone. Some species are quite talkative, while others are known to be cuddlers, and still others are playful clowns.

Conures are notorious chewers, and many have quite loud voices. They enjoy regular baths. Some species are noted for sleeping on their backs with their feet in the air, while others tend to be feather pickers.

Conures need roomy cages in which to exercise and play. Of course, they need out-of-cage time, too, which can be spent on a play gym or with their owners. A good-quality seed mix or pellets, supplemented with fresh foods, makes an adequate conure diet.

Diamond Doves

Diamond doves are native to Australia. They take their name from the pattern of small white dots that is found across their otherwise gray wings. About a dozen color forms exist besides the wild gray form, including cinnamon, red diamond, yellow diamond and snow white.

Diamond doves can be housed with small finches in community aviaries. A pair of birds can also be kept in a roomy cage. They eat a variety of grass seeds, supplemented with moistened cornbread or well-cooked hard-boiled eggs. Diamond doves will also eat chopped green food if it is offered.

Diamond doves are prolific breeders in captivity. Chicks hatch after a two-week incubation period, and they can leave the nest 10 days after hatching. Sexes can be determined when the chicks are about 6 weeks old, and the young birds are capable of breeding when they are about 5 months of age.

Eclectus

Eclectus are large, solid parrots from the South Pacific. They are not usually cuddly parrots and seem to prefer sitting on their owners' hands or on a perch near their owners.

Some eclectus may pick their feathers. Females can be moody during breeding season after they become sexually mature at about 4 years of age. Females are traditionally more aggressive than males.

Eclectus have different vitamin A requirements than other parrot species. Ask your avian veterinarian for suggestions on the best diet for your eclectus.

Provide these parrots with large cages and time-out on a play gym or with you to keep them content.

Finches

Finches are small, active cage birds that come from Asia, Africa and Australia. They are well suited to community aviaries or flights, although a pair or a single pet finch can easily be kept in a cage.

Some species are noted for their colorful feathers, while others sing pleasant songs. Finches are often admired from afar, rather than being cuddled and held by their owners, although some may learn to enjoy sitting on their owners' shoulders.

In aviary settings, finches may have their feathers picked by cagemates. If you find a picked finch, you may have to remove it from the aviary in order to allow its feathers to grow back.

Grass Parakeets

Grass parakeet is a term used to describe several genera of small, colorful Australian parrots that make good candidates for aviary living. They can be kept with finches and small, nonaggressive parrots. Commonly kept species include the Bourke's parakeet, the Princess of Wales parakeet and the red-rumped parakeet.

Grass parakeets are noted for their high activity levels and their quiet voices. They do not need regular interaction with people to feel content. Because they are strong fliers and need to exercise their wings, grass parakeets need large flights or aviaries.

Grass parakeets enjoy a mixture of grass seeds in their diet. These can be supplemented with greens, apples, corn, broccoli and carrots. Some species also relish a bean-and-rice mixture.

Many species of grass parakeets are sexually dimorphic: The males generally display brighter, more colorful plumage than the females.

Hawkheaded Parrots

Hawkheaded parrots are colorful medium-sized parrots from South America. They are playful, somewhat shy parrots prone to feather picking if stressed.

The hawkhead's plumage is its most notable feature. The birds have brown faces, green wings and red chest and neck feathers that are tipped in blue. These birds have the ability to raise their neck feathers to the point that the feathers form a ruff around the bird's face. Experts theorize that this behavior developed as a defensive mechanism in the wild. The ruff may also be raised when the birds are exceptionally happy.

Hawkheads are capable of mimicking sounds and whistles, and some may learn to say a few words. They require a varied diet of seeds and fresh foods, daily attention and mental stimulation, such as toys, to be content pets. They should be housed in good-sized cages.

Kakarikis

Kakarikis (pronounced kak-uh-REE-kees) are small, highly active parrots from New Zealand. Their name derives from a Maori word for "little parrot." They are bold birds that have no real fear of people. They are not naturally cuddly, and some individuals may be high strung.

Two kakariki species are available in the United States: the red-fronted kakariki and the yellow-crowned kakariki. In both species, the birds are predominantly green with either red or yellow feathers on their heads.

Kakarikis are also highly curious birds. They will investigate their environments completely, so care must be taken to parrot-proof any area to which a kakariki has access.

Because of their active natures, kakarikis need large cages. Unlike other parrots, their food bowls should be placed on the bottom of their cages because kakarikis will dig around in their food bowls. Their diets should include a good-quality seed mix, supplemented with fresh foods.

Lories

Lories are active, lively parrots from the South Pacific. They are available in a variety of sizes and colors to suit almost anyone's taste. Keep in mind that these brush-tongued parrots are specialty feeders, favoring a diet of nectar and fruit over seeds.

Some lory species are likely to talk, and all are willing and able to play. Lories like to sleep in nest boxes even when they aren't breeding, so they will need to have an enclosed sleeping space attached to their cages. A play gym or a cage top play area is also recommended for these acrobatic birds.

Lories enjoy frequent baths and may bathe in their water bowls. Their fruit-and-nectar-based diets cause them to produce messy droppings, although powdered forms of diet are available that make lory keeping easier. They are not recommended for first-time bird keepers.

Lovebirds

Lovebirds are energetic little parrots from Africa and Madagascar. They are available in a variety of colors, including blue, green, and yellow and green.

Despite their seemingly cuddly name, lovebirds can be downright aggressive toward other birds and people. Hand-fed birds, which are easier to tame than parent-raised birds, require daily handling to retain their sweet pet qualities. Bird owners who want to admire their pets from afar may fare better with a less-tame pair in an aviary or flight.

Lovebirds are prone to chewing and particularly enjoy ripping up paper. They may also pick their feathers.

Although they're little birds, lovebirds need good-sized cages because they like to climb and exercise. You'll also have to provide your lovebirds with toys, which will be another outlet for these parrots' seemingly endless energy. Feed your lovebirds a good-quality seed mix supplemented with fresh fruits and vegetables.

Macaws

Macaws are the largest commonly kept cage birds. They hail from South America and are available in a rainbow of colors, including green, blue and red.

Macaws are highly intelligent, outgoing birds that can learn to talk or to perform tricks. They can be quite destructive in their chewing habits, so be sure to provide these large parrots with plenty of destroyable toys. They are also prone to fits of screaming that makes them unsuitable for apartment living.

Macaws can be aggressive during breeding season and can intimidate some owners with their beaks and their strong wills. Macaws require large cages in order to be healthy and mentally well adjusted. The larger macaws are not recommended for first-time bird owners.

Diets for macaws should include a good-quality seed mix or pellets, supplemented with fresh fruits and vegetables. Nuts can be offered as treats, and they will keep your macaws entertained and busy as the birds crack the nuts.

Mynahs

Mynahs are social birds that need regular human companionship. They are among the most renowned mimics in the avian world and are capable of imitating a wide range of voices, intonations and sounds. In keeping with these charming characteristics, however, they can also be quite loud, especially before bedtime.

Mynahs require large cages in order to exercise regularly. They are not always good candidates for a community aviary because they may not get along well with smaller birds.

As a softbill, a mynah relies on a large amount of insects and fruits in its diet, as opposed to the seed-based diet most parrots eat. Mynahs are not among the neatest eaters in the animal kingdom and, as a result, require a regular post-meal cleanup to keep your home and their health in tip-top shape. Their fruit-based diets cause them to produce liquid droppings that can be messy. They may be prone to iron storage disease (hemachromatosis), which is an often fatal liver problem that is caused by feeding the birds a diet that contains too much iron.

Mynahs can be trained to sit on their owners' hands, but they prefer to sit on a flat palm rather than a pair of fingers or a loosely clenched fist. Mynahs need to have their nails trimmed regularly, but wing trimming is not recommended because mynahs can crash and injure themselves if their wings are clipped. As a result, you must be extremely careful that all windows and doors are closed tightly whenever your mynah is out of its cage.

Mynahs like to sit on their owners' shoulders and preen their owners' hair and faces. During the course of a normal day, a mynah is liable to yawn, stretch, scratch, sneeze, preen, nap, eat and drink.

Parrotlets

Parrotlets are small, predominantly green birds from Latin America. These spunky little birds have large personalities and are well suited to living in small spaces, such as apartments or mobile homes.

Parrotlets are bold little birds. They enjoy human companionship and are very active. If allowed out of their cage, the birds will play busily on a play gym.

Because parrotlets are so bold, they need close supervision when they are out of their cages to ensure their safety. They can be prone to feather picking. They can be housed in medium-sized cages and should be fed a good-quality seed mixture supplemented with fresh fruits and vegetables.

Pekin Robins

Pekin robins, also called Chinese nightingales, are softbills that are often kept in aviaries or community flights. They are found in the wild in several countries in Asia, and they were introduced to Hawaii, where they can now be found in the wild.

Pekin robins are rather drab in their plumage, but they sing beautiful songs. The male's song has been described as lilting, strong and sweet. They are active, inquisitive birds that should be kept in pairs because they are birds that practice contact sitting and roost close to one another.

In captivity, the pekin robin's diet should include commercial softbill diets—greens and live food, such as mealworms, aphids or white worms. You can also offer apples, oranges, bananas, grapes or blueberries. These birds should be housed in large cages or put into community flights with finches.

Pionus

Pionus (pronounced pie-OH-nus) are generally quiet, curious birds that come from Latin America. These medium-sized, chunky parrots enjoy bathing and climbing, and they are noted for their chewing abilities. Pionus have gentle, even temperaments.

Pionus enjoy human companionship, but they do not need to be handled and cuddled in order to be content. Their size and quiet natures make them ideal for apartment dwellers.

Pionus may wheeze when excited, and they can be high-strung and some-what nervous. They do not tolerate heat and/or humidity well and may become stressed easily.

Pionus socialize well and are good choices for first parrots. They need to be housed in large cages and fed a good-quality seed mixture or pellets, supplemented with fresh foods.

Quaker Parrots

Quaker or monk parrots are from South America. These small parrots are available in a variety of colors, including green, lutino (yellow) and blue.

Quakers can develop large vocabularies, and they are also capable of learning to do tricks. They are chunky, active little birds that need adequate space in which to exercise. Quakers enjoy a daily bath.

Quakers can be aggressive toward other birds and humans who invade their space. They can also become possessive of their favorite person in the home. Keeping Quakers is illegal in some states because they are perceived as an agricultural threat if they escape.

Quakers should be housed in large cages and provided with plenty of toys. They should be fed a good-quality seed mix or pellets, supplemented with fresh fruits and vegetables.

Ringnecked Parakeets

Ringnecked parakeets are slender, long-tailed birds that hail from Africa and Asia. They take their name from the thin ring of feathers around their necks. Most birds are bright green, but blue and lutino (yellow) mutations are available.

The personalities of the ringnecked parakeets differs slightly among the species. Indian ringnecks are comical, while Alexandrines are more serious. Plumheads are talkative little scamps, while slatyheads are sweet, quiet birds. Some species are sexually dimorphic, which means the males and females have different plumage, while others are not.

Broadly, ringnecks enjoy attention more than they like being handled. Ringnecks can develop sizable vocabularies, and they can learn to perform tricks. These active parrots need large cages in which to exercise and to protect their plumage from damage. Their diets should include a good-quality seed mix supplemented with fresh fruits and vegetables.

Rosellas

Rosellas are small, colorful parrots from Australia. They are predominantly known as aviary subjects, but they can also be kept as single pet birds. Rosella owners must realize that these birds are not naturally cuddly birds and like their space. Some birds can be pugnacious.

Eight species of rosella have been recognized in aviculture. Each species has well-defined white or yellow cheek patches and a scalloped pattern on the back.

Rosellas need to be housed in large cages or aviaries. They are active fliers and need regular opportunities to exercise. Offer them a good-quality seed mix and some fresh foods to eat.

Senegals

Senegals are small African parrots from the *Poicephalus* genus that also includes Jardine's, Meyer's and red-bellied parrots. Senegals may learn to talk and can perform tricks. They are noted for their chewing ability.

Some Senegals may become nippy after they are weaned, and they can be strong-willed pets. Their small size and relatively low noise level make them good candidates for apartment living.

Senegals can be housed in medium-sized cages, and they should be provided with a variety of toys. Their diet should include a good-quality seed mix or pellets, supplemented with fresh foods.

Tanygnathus

Tanygnathus (pronounced tan-IG-nay-thus) parrots are found in the Philippine Islands and Indonesia. The genus includes the great-billed parrot, Muller's parrot and the blue-naped parrot.

Tanygnathus are predominantly green birds with reddish or coral-colored beaks. In this genus, females tend to be more dominant than males, and therefore male birds may make better pets.

Tanygnathus love frequent baths, so owners must provide opportunities for their birds to bathe. They are also noted for their chewing ability, and they need an ample supply of chewable toys.

A good-quality seed mix and some fresh foods should provide an adequate diet for *Tanygnathus*. They need to be housed in large cages.

Toucans

Toucans are medium-sized softbills from Latin America. Some birds are highly territorial. Their calls, which have been compared to howler monkeys at the zoo, can be irritating to some people.

The toucan's most striking feature is its bill, which is surprisingly lightweight and contains a honeycomb-like structure inside it. Toucans are unable to use their beaks to chew, but with some work they can crush grapes in their beaks. Although the beak is not as useful as a parrot's, it still presents a formidable weapon. If a toucan bites, its beak can be hard to remove from a finger or ear.

Some toucans require live food, such as small rodents, but much of their diet is made up of fruit. Toucans are prone to hemachromatosis, an often fatal liver disease that results from being fed a diet too rich in iron.

These birds also need to live in large aviaries or flights because they need a lot of exercise. Toucan keepers should know that these birds are infinitely curious about their surroundings and will explore an enclosure thoroughly. Toucans will try to eat almost anything they can get their beaks on, so their aviaries or flights will need to be toucan-proofed for their safety. Toucans are not recommended for first-time bird keepers.

Touracos

Touracos are fruit eaters that come from Africa. These crested softbills can be housed in community aviaries, but, because they are very active, they need a large aviary or flight.

Touracos are seldom aggressive toward other species of birds, but they can treat their mates roughly during breeding season. They build flimsy nests and lay two eggs. Parent birds share incubation duties, and the eggs hatch after a 21-day incubation. Hand-fed chicks make devoted pets. These birds are demanding pets and are not recommended for first-time bird keepers.

RESOURCES

Recommended Reading

About Bird Behavior

Alderton, David. *You and Your Pet Bird.* New York: Alfred A. Knopf, 1994.

————. *A Birdkeeper's Guide to Cockatoos.* Blacksburg, VA: Tetra Press, 1990.

————. *A Birdkeeper's Guide to Cockatiels.* Blacksburg, VA: Tetra Press, 1989.

————. *A Birdkeeper's Guide to Parrots and Macaws.* Blacksburg, VA: Tetra Press, 1989.

————. *A Birdkeeper's Guide to Budgies.* Blacksburg, VA: Tetra Press, 1988.

————. *A Birdkeeper's Guide to Finches.* Blacksburg, VA: Tetra Press, 1988.

————. *A Birdkeeper's Guide to Pet Birds.* Blacksburg, VA: Tetra Press, 1987.

————. *The Complete Guide to Bird Care.* New York: Howell Book House, 1998.

Barber, Theodore X. PhD. *The Human Nature of Birds.* New York: St. Martin's Press, 1993.

Birmelin, Immanuel, and Annette Wolter. *The New Parakeet Handbook.* Hauppauge, NY: Barron's Educational Series, Inc., 1986.

Doane, Bonnie Munro, and Thomas Qualkinbush. *My Parrot, My Friend: An Owner's Guide to Parrot Behavior.* New York: Howell Book House, 1994.

Forshaw, Joseph. *Parrots of the World.* Neptune, NJ: TFH Publications Inc., 1977.

Freud, Arthur. *The Parrot: An Owner's Guide to a Happy, Healthy Pet.* New York: Howell Book House, 1996.

Griffin, Donald R. *Animal Minds.* Chicago: University of Chicago Press, 1992.

Hanna, Jack and Hester Mundis. *Jack Hanna's Ultimate Guide to Pets.* New York: G.P. Putnam's Sons, 1996.

Koepff, Christa. *The New Finch Handbook.* Hauppauge, NY: Barron's Educational Series, Inc., 1984.

Lantermann, Werner, and Susanne Lanterman. *Cockatoos: A Complete Pet Owner's Manual.* Hauppauge, NY: Barron's Educational Series, Inc., 1989.

Lantermann, Werner. *The New Parrot Handbook.* Hauppauge, NY: Barron's Educational Series, Inc., 1986.

Masson, Jeffrey M., and Susan McCarthy. *When Elephants Weep: The Emotional Lives of Animals.* New York: Delacorte Press, 1995.

McClung, Robert M. *Lost Wild America: The Story of Our Extinct and Vanishing Wildlife.* Hamden, CT: Linnett Books, 1993.

Morton, Eugene S., and Jake Page. *Animal Talk: Science and the Voices of Nature.* New York: Random House, 1992.

Paradise, Paul. *Canaries.* Neptune, NJ: TFH Publications, 1979.

Randolph, Elizabeth. *The Basic Bird Book.* New York: Fawcett Crest, 1989.

Reed, Nancy A. *Cockatiels! Pet—Breeding—Showing.* Neptune, NJ: TFH Publications Inc., 1990.

Rogers, Cyril H. *Zebra Finches: The Bird Keeper's Library.* Edinburgh: K & R Books Ltd., 1979.

Short, Lester L. *The Lives of Birds: Birds of the World and Their Behavior.* New York: Henry Holt and Co., 1993.

Sutherland, Patricia. *The Pet Bird Handbook.* New York: Arco Publishing, 1981.

von Frisch, Otto. *Mynahs: A Complete Pet Owner's Manual.* Hauppauge, NY: Barron's Educational Series, Inc., 1986.

———. *Canaries: Everything About Purchase, Care, Diseases, Nutrition and Song.* Hauppauge, NY: Barron's Educational Series, Inc., 1983.

Vriends, Matthew M. Ph.D. *The New Cockatiel Handbook.* Hauppauge, NY: Barron's Educational Series, Inc., 1989.

———. *The Complete Book of Finches.* New York: Howell Book House, 1987.

──── *Lovebirds: A Complete Pet Owner's Manual.* Hauppauge, NY: Barron's Educational Series, Inc., 1986.

Wolter, Annette. *Cockatiels: A Complete Pet Owner's Manual.* Hauppauge, NY: Barron's Educational Series, Inc., 1991.

────. *African Gray Parrots: A Complete Pet Owner's Manual.* Hauppauge, NY: Barron's Educational Series Inc., 1987.

About Behaviors that Indicate Illness

Doane, Bonnie Munro. *The Parrot in Health and Illness: An Owner's Guide.* New York: Howell Book House, 1991.

Gallerstein, Gary A. DVM. *The Complete Bird Owner's Handbook.* New York: Howell Book House, 1994.

Ritchie, Branson W. DVM, PhD, Greg J. Harrison, DVM, and Linda R. Harrison. *Avian Medicine: Principles and Application.* Lake Worth, FL: Wingers Publishing Inc., 1994.

About Breeding Behaviors

Gonzalez, Fran. *Breeding Exotic Birds: A Beginner's Guide.* Cypress, CA: Neon Pet Publications, 1993.

Schubot, Richard, Susan Clubb, DVM, and Kevin Clubb. *Psittacine Aviculture.* Loxahatchee, FL: Avicultural Breeding and Research Center, 1992.

About Training

Athan, Mattie Sue. *Guide to a Well-Behaved Parrot.* Hauppauge, NY: Barron's Educational Series, Inc., 1993.

Hubbard, Jennifer. *The New Parrot Training Handbook.* Fremont, CA: Parrot Press, 1997.

Murphy, Kevin. *Training Your Parrot.* Neptune, NJ: TFH Publications Inc., 1983.

Magazines/Newsletters

Bird Talk
P.O. Box 57347
Boulder, CO 80322-7347

Bird Times
7-L Dundas Circle
Greensboro, NC 27499-0765

Birds USA
Look for it in your local bookstore or pet store.

Pet Bird Report
2236 Mariner Square Drive #35W
Alameda, CA 94501

Online Resources

Bird-specific sites have been cropping up regularly on the Internet. These sites offer pet bird owners the opportunity to share stories about their pets, along with trading helpful hints about bird care.

If you belong to an online service, look for the pet site (it is often included in more general topics, such as "Hobbies and Interests," or more specifically "Pets"). If you have Internet access, ask your Web browser software to search for "bird behavior" or "parrot behavior."

Organizations

The following associations are interested in avian health and behavior.

American Animal Hospital Association
P.O. Box 150899
Denver, CO 80215-0899

American College of Veterinary Behaviorists
Dept. of Small Animal Medicine and Surgery
Texas A&M University
College Station, TX 77843-4474

American Federation of Aviculture
P.O. Box 56218
Phoenix, AZ 85079-6128

American Veterinary Medical Association
1931 N. Meacham Rd.
Suite 100
Schaumburg, IL 60173

Association of Avian Veterinarians
P.O. Box 811720
Boca Raton, FL 33481

Avicultural Society of America
P.O. Box 5516
Riverside, CA 92517-5517

International Avicultural Society
P.O. Box 280383
Memphis, TN 38168

Parrot Rehabilitation Society
P.O. Box 620213
San Diego, CA 92612-0213

Society of Parrot Breeders and Exhibitors
P.O. Box 369
Groton, MA 01450

U.S. World Parrot Trust
P.O. Box 341141
Memphis, TN 38184

Videos

The Positive Approach to Parrots as Pets: Understanding Bird Behavior (tape 1)
and *Training Through Positive Reinforcement* (tape 2). Natural Encounters Inc.,
P.O. Box 68666, Indianapolis, IN 46268.

INDEX